MW01128069

Trout Unlimited's Guide to
Pennsylvania
Limestone Streams

Trout Unlimited's Guide to
Pennsylvania Limestone Streams

A. Joseph Armstrong

STACKPOLE
BOOKS

Copyright © 1992 by Stackpole Books

Published by STACKPOLE BOOKS
Cameron and Kelker Streets
P.O. Box 1831
Harrisburg, PA 17105

Printed in the United States of America

10 9 8 7 6 5 4 3 2 1

First edition

Cover design by Mark B. Olszewski
Maps by Donna Ziegenfuss
Line drawings by Ann Armstrong

Library of Congress Cataloging-in-Publication Data

Armstrong, A. Joseph.
   Trout Unlimited's guide to Pennsylvania limestone
streams / A. Joseph Armstrong.
      p.   cm.
   ISBN 0-8117-1651-1
   1. Trout fishing—Pennsylvania—Guide-books.
2. Rivers—Pennsylvania—Guide-books.
3. Pennsylvania—Description and travel—1981—Guide-
books. I. Trout Unlimited. II. Title. III. Title: Pennsylvania
limestone streams. IV. Title: Limestone streams.
SH688.U6A76   1992
799.1'755—dc20   91-34271
                                                            CIP

To the landowners
whose responsible land stewardship
ensures high-quality trout-stream habitat.
With their permission we have access
to the streams we love so much.

The highest good is that of water.
The goodness of water is that it benefits
Ten thousand creatures, yet itself does not wrangle,
But is content with the places that all men disdain.
It is this that makes water so near the Tao.

That the yielding conquers the resistant
and the soft conquers the hard
is a fact known by all men
yet utilized by none.

Lao Tzu
Fifth Century B.C.

Contents

Acknowledgments

The title of this book is *Trout Unlimited's Guide to Pennsylvania Limestone Streams*. Then why is there so much first person singular in it? The ubiquitous "I" simply means that I actually visited each stream. The observations are mine, and they clearly show what I experienced. They also show what I missed. All errors, omissions, and outrageous statements are solely mine, and any goofs should come back to my doorstep. But there were many people who made tremendous contributions to this book. They directed me to places I had missed, pointed out local hatches, and set me straight on misinterpretations. Without them the whole project simply wouldn't have flown, and they deserve considerable thanks and praise for taking their time to move this effort ahead.

The Pennsylvania Fish Commission helped in many ways, as an organization and as individuals. We are very fortunate to have such a thoroughly professional agency to work with on those matters that affect our trout fisheries.

Many people within the Trout Unlimited (TU) community provided appreciated insights and corrections to this work. Joe Kohler, Marcia Drass, Don Baylor, George Myers, Norman Conrad, Charles Boettcher, Ann Baines, Larry Hartlaub, Dan Shields, Steve Sywensky, Dick Tietbohl, Charlie Meck, Frank Nale, Dr. John Hampsey, and John Childe all provided much-needed comments on various aspects of the work. Mark Nale gave me some very helpful suggestions as well as photographs for the cover. Paul Nale and Bill Kodrich read through the manuscript and contributed helpful comments as to what was missing and how to make the work more useful to the reader. Don Douple slogged through the manuscript and pointed out numerous problems needing attention. Judith Schnell and John Cominsky of Stackpole Books did yeoman service pulling the whole mess together to make a presentable piece of work.

Finally, my incredibly patient wife put up with this effort through what seems an eternity. It's hard to say which one of us is more pleased that it is now wrapped up. For the first time in some years the dining room table will be available for such unlikely uses as dinner. Her sketches give life to what otherwise may have been stiff going.

All the people mentioned here deserve many thanks for their varied contributions.

A.J. Armstrong

Introduction

In 1980 the Valley Forge Chapter of Trout Unlimited became involved with water-quality standards, which are set for each stream or stream segment in the Commonwealth by the Pennsylvania Department of Environmental Resources (DER). They had designated our home stream—West Valley Creek, a nice little limestone stream—as a "trout-stocking fishery." This designation provides protection for a stocked trout population until mid-summer, when, presumably, all the fish have disappeared. Since there are no trout left to protect, water temperatures may be raised legally by industrial or other effluents to levels above the lethal limits for trout. However, since we knew there were trout in our stream throughout the year, we launched an effort to get it redesignated as the more stringent "cold-water fishery," which gives thermal and other protection year-round.

Some years later we did the same thing on another local limestone stream with the similar name of Valley Creek. Both of these streams had been classified incorrectly, both were good fisheries, and both were limestone streams. This raised the question, which seemed logical at the time, "How many other limestone streams have been misclassified?"

That deceptively simple question set this project in motion. I knew there were maybe thirty-five to fifty such streams, so I set out to fish them all, to see if corrections were needed, to write up the results of the odyssey, and to try to sell the book, with the proceeds to go to the Pennsylvania Council of Trout Unlimited.

The number and diversity of truly excellent streams, as well as how widespread they are, were constant sources of wonder to me. Initially I thought that there were at most fifty such streams, mostly in Cumberland County, a few others in Lehigh and Northampton counties, and maybe one or two in Centre County and the immediate surroundings. If I had known at the beginning just how numerous and widespread the streams are, I don't think this project would have ever gotten off the ground. By the time I realized the size of this undertaking, however, things were well enough along that it seemed reasonable to continue. I told myself that, with so much time already invested, I might as well stick with it and finish up the next summer. And each summer I went back.

I ended up fishing a very large number of limestone streams. I also had the thrill of discovering new and seemingly unknown limestone gems. The results of my research and my discoveries are reported here.

Although I did discover—and have commented on—several problem areas, I'm pleased to say I did not find many streams that were incorrectly designated.

These limestoners are special waters: unusual streams with unique fish. Come along and see what Pennsylvania has to offer in the way of limestone streams, and help Trout Unlimited protect them for future generations.

PART ONE

THE LIMESTONE

METHODOLOGY

It was immediately apparent that if I wanted to fish all the limestone streams in the Commonwealth, I would have to be able to locate them, and that would involve geologic maps. Fortunately they are available.

In the earliest days of the project I worked out a series of cross-checks between the different information sources. My basic reference was the "Pennsylvania Geological Survey Mineral Resource Report 50," which maps the limestone and dolomite deposits (and nothing else) in the state. This showed the best deposits to be in the central and southeastern parts of the Commonwealth and made it quite easy to figure out where to start looking. Next I turned to the "Stream Map of Pennsylvania," published by Penn State, which showed what streams were in the areas of limestone outcrops located above. The two maps were drawn to different scales and showed different towns, but between them I was able to get a good idea of what was likely to be in a particular area.

The Pennsylvania Fish Commission publishes their excellent "Trout Fishing in Pennsylvania," a series of stream maps that forms the basis for the maps used in this book. These show trout waters and indicate which are wild trout waters and which are stocked. This is very helpful information to know before venturing forth.

A fourth map, a family heirloom, is grandly titled "A Map of Pennsylvania Exhibiting not only the Improved Parts of that Province but also its Extensive Frontiers, laid down from Actual Surveys and Chiefly from the late Map of W. Scull published in 1770, and Humbly Inscribed to the Honourable Thomas Penn and Richard Penn Esquires, True and Absolute Proprietaries and Governors of the Province of Pennsylvania and the Territories Thereunto Belonging." This map was published in June of 1775 and is fascinating, showing the seven counties then in existence, as well as an excellent knowledge of streams all across the state. It had a particular way of showing large springs that was very helpful. It showed, for instance, Centre County's Spring Creek, Clinton County's Fishing Creek, and Centre, Mifflin, Union, and Snyder counties' Penns Creek, all named and displayed quite accurately. The counties themselves weren't there, but the streams, along with many others, were apparently well known.

The Pennsylvania Department of Environmental Resources (DER) publishes a list of all the streams in the Commonwealth by basin. Once I understood their system, it provided insight into which streams were where, as some didn't show up on maps, especially the smaller ones. In other cases, maps sometimes showed a stream but deleted the name, so that list provided a great cross-check.

The Fish Commission's list of Class A wild trout waters and a list of streams proposed for upgrading under the DER's water-classification system also provided valuable input.

Fairly late in the game it occurred to me that maybe I was off base and that limestone bedrock alone might not be enough to characterize a stream since the imprint might not be as large as I had assumed. The anomaly of Weir and Pohopoco creeks in Monroe County cast doubts on my basic premise. According to my map, there was no limestone there, but the streams appeared to be limestone in most characteristics. A search ensued to see if other writers had tried to relate stream water quality to underlying geology. Fortunately, an article by Bricker and Rice on this subject turned up in *Environmental Science and Technology*. They addressed the ability, based on the bedrock, of a number of central Maryland streams (immediately adjacent to Adams County in Pennsylvania) to cope with acid rain and found those streams in limestone areas to be high in alkali content (pH) and have excellent buffering capacity, while the nearby freestone streams did not. In essence, those streams that flowed over limestone were, in fact, limestone streams.

Other sources of information were the bits and pieces gleaned from anyone I could buttonhole. Some paradoxes were explained this way, and some streams that had totally slipped through my sifting procedure were pinpointed.

All of these sources provided information for me to compare in order to prepare my lists, which were growing steadily. Nevertheless, all of the comparing and listing were not enough to nail down details of where the streams were and how best to get there. Fortunately, at exactly the right time, the *Pennsylvania Atlas and Gazetteer*, published by DeLorme, appeared. A series of topographical maps of the entire state showing the details of roads, hills, and valleys in minute detail, these made the actual visits to the streams infinitely easier.

Armed with all this information, I planned my outings. I discovered I could visit from my home near West Chester a surprising number of streams during long midsummer evenings. Longer ventures involved weekends. Since some planning was needed to make these longer forays more efficient, I worked out a procedure. First I picked a county—one of the "good counties" if it was likely to be a time of heavy hatches, a lesser area if it was midsummer—and examined the list of streams and compared it to the various maps. Then I worked out a sequence to get from one stream to the next with minimal backtracking. Often it was clear that some streams were best visited when fishing an adjacent county, and these were deleted from the list for that weekend. To the extent possible, the evenings and early mornings were designated to fish what appeared to be the best streams in the area, and midday was set aside for the less-inviting streams. Contingencies were worked out as well, since I knew thunderstorms could often wipe out one area but leave nearby areas unscathed. Eventually, I came up with an impossibly long list.

The first thing I did upon arriving at a stream site was to drive around to get some idea about the area. I tried to keep in mind the limits of the limestone outcrops while I visited other sites on or downstream from the limestone area. Not only did this give me a general feel for the stream, it also gave me a feel for what might be more-inviting or less-inviting water. Typically, I also took a few water-temperature readings—and the air temperature to give it context—during this general reconnaissance. This procedure sorted things out in a hurry, since quite often there would be an area where there was a clear-cut jolt of cold water or other limestone influence. I also took notes on insect hatches that were in evidence (in the air, as nymphal shucks on the rocks, in cobwebs, or other places), the presence or lack of stream vegetation, and the general nature of the area.

Additionally, an effort was made to determine which streams might logically be considered part of a "fishery."

Once I had things narrowed down, I selected an area well away from the road. I can't emphasize enough how important this is: if catching a lot of fish is the goal, don't stay right beside the road. In a few instances I found some good fishing near factories that were built along the streams, presumably because most fishermen stay away from man-made sites.

Actual fishing, at least from midmorning through evening, almost invariably involved putting on a size 16 Ausable Wulff since this was mainly an exercise in trying to catch brown trout, and that pattern seems to be the equivalent of brown-trout candy. It has proven to be effective for me time after time. This is not to say that I caught every fish present, but it did give me a pretty good idea about the things I needed to know: whether there was much of a trout population, in what size ranges, and whether or not they were wild. In early mornings, nymphing was the call, typically with a size 14 Hare's Ear or a weighted woven-body nymph. Again, the fly clearly didn't take every fish in the stream, but I came away with a pretty good idea of what the trout population was like. Most of the time I found I had a good feel for the streams, although occasionally I decided to revisit a few.

Normally, fishing was done over a half mile of stream, but this varied widely with conditions. If a stream turned out to be a dry bed, then naturally that was that. Similarly, if the water was warm, above 80 degrees Fahrenheit (all temperatures in this book are quoted in Fahrenheit), then no effort was made to look further, since this would not be trout water.

On really long streams, fishing was sampled along the length, but no effort was made to fish every inch of it. This would not be appropriate anyway, since many of the streams listed have relatively short stretches where they cross limestone.

Generally, I found that small streams have great charm. This point of view is not universally shared, but I rarely dropped a stream from my search for being too small. In some cases the stream was wide enough but it was quite short—until it connected with larger water. In others the narrowness made it appear insignificant. But I knew about a local jewel—with an average width of about 6 feet—with a population of about one wild trout per running foot of stream, so I wasn't about to ignore the smaller streams.

One other major source of information was simply keeping my eyes open while driving around. As a result, I've been able to include a number of lovely waters that for various reasons did not show up on the maps but which are an important part of this project. It was a real joy to stumble upon an unknown and uncharted stream full of rising wild trout.

After fishing, I immediately wrote up my notes. If questions arose, another stretch might be tried or an effort made to verify what was observed. Once everything was written up, I asked someone in the area—typically, the local TU chapter president—to read it. After this was done, the information was reviewed once more to make certain nothing had slipped between the cracks. Doubtless some streams have gone unnoticed—there are so many out there—but the main thrust of my methodology was to minimize their number.

LIMESTONE

It is impossible to imagine how it was many millions of years ago in Precambrian times when these oldest limestone deposits were laid down. The climate was much harsher then, but some scientists think the limestone was laid down as part of a natural mellowing of previous greenhouse-effect eras. The deposits are often hundreds, sometimes thousands, of feet thick, but they are not petroliferous, so some of the worst aspects of oil and gas production do not accompany them. They are not crucial to heavy industry, so pastoral would be the best description for most of the limestone areas of the state. The land is far too productive for any true wilderness to still exist, but, in general, major congestion is also mercifully absent.

Limestone is soluble in acidic water. Caves are one manifestation of this, as are the less impressive but much more widely spread sinkholes that dot most limestone areas. These sinkholes, in effect, are entrances to small caverns, and the caverns produce large areas for water flow. Limestone areas are well known for their prolific springs and wells. The water is very hard, there is a lot of it, and it is cold. The hardness comes from dissolved nutrients, which the food chain efficiently converts to trout flesh.

Limestone and closely related dolomite come in many colors and textures. Some of the formations are thin and shaley, while others are massive and sometimes as much as eleven thousand feet thick. Ages vary from Precambrian, the dawn of life on earth, up to the more recent Triassic, the time when dinosaurs galumphed across the landscape.

Paul Nale pointed out a fascinating relationship between life and limestone that is worth passing along. In Precambrian times, several billion years ago, cyanobacteria started decarbonating the water. This created oxygen, and slowly but surely the atmosphere as we know it evolved. Limestone is a by-product of this process—that is, life made limestone, and limestone made life. There is reason to believe that limestone might be unique to earth, and that adds a more profound meaning to its effects on our streams.

Groundwater, which is crucial to streams, generally is found in the upper one hundred or so feet of the limestone, with water yields diminishing rapidly with depth. In a few areas of extreme southeastern Pennsylvania, limestone of ancient age has been metamorphosed into marble. A few of these deposits have positively influenced some Chester County streams, although on a statewide basis it is the unmetamorphosed deposits that give the streams, and their whole ecosystems, their character.

LIMESTONE STREAMS

Limestone. Mention it to a trout fisherman and you'll set off a flood of associations—exquisitely clear pictures in sharp focus flashing like a slide show in fast forward. Watercress. Dimples. Blizzardlike hatches. Seductive currents. Fat trout!

Well, just what is a limestone stream? Why does it elicit this extraordinary response?

Any stream can be classified as either freestone or limestone. Freestone streams are much more widespread than limestone streams. They are typically fed by a myriad of small seeps that eventually merge to form the stream. Alkalinity (dissolved minerals) is low, swings between winter and summer temperatures are normally wide, and aquatic vegetation is relatively rare. But waterfalls, pocket water, and the various attributes of wilderness trout streams are frequently present. The low alkalinity means that the stream is ill prepared to deal with acid rain, and although there are some marvelous freestone stream fisheries, in general they represent a harsher environment than limestone streams.

Limestone streams are made up of the flow from large springs, which yields large amounts of constant-temperature, mineral-rich waters. The large flow of constant-temperature water means there is not much variation in temperature through the year. The streams run warmer in winter and colder in summer than their freestone counterparts. The high-mineral content of the water is reflected in a high pH, which in turn means that threats such as acid rain are easily dealt with since the stream simply neutralizes the acidity of the rain. This is termed buffering capacity, and in effect means that the stream carries out naturally the same process accomplished by an antacid tablet.

The high-alkali content has another highly beneficial effect. These dissolved minerals are nutrients for a wide variety of life forms. Aquatic vegetation is often plentiful and provides the basis for an abundant food chain as well as hiding places for all manner of stream life, including the trout. Much of the invertebrate life of the stream survives in or around this vegetation. Cress bugs and freshwater shrimp are often abundant and can be choice food for the most selective trout, as are the nymphs of many aquatic insects which later emerge in plentiful hatches. However, these dense beds of aquatic vegetation often trap considerable amounts of silt, and in late summer, when weed growth is heavy, they can force the stream from its banks. Spring creeks—those limestoners fed by large springs—of-

10 PENNSYLVANIA LIMESTONE STREAMS

ten are not subject to high-water flood events that might flush out such silt.

One of the most important aspects of all this is that these streams form almost ideal trout habitat. They are veritable trout factories, with some astonishingly high populations. Being warm in winter but cold in summer, without the stresses of floods or acid spikes at spring runoff and with plenty to eat, these streams combine all the right factors to produce truly exceptional fisheries.

Spring creeks are the purest form of limestone streams. They are fed by one or a few very large springs and are typified by sedate (and seductive) currents with very little vertical drop. They have lush aquatic vegetation and few of the typical pool-and-riffle arrangements of a normal stream. The nearly constant temperature helps produce abundant life. There is plenty to eat and lots of places for trout to hide from predators and each other. In these spring creeks, the trout grow large and there are many of them.

Many other streams are fed by substantial springs, which gives them the high alkalinity and constant temperature of a spring creek, but they have sufficient vertical drop to have the pool-and-riffle arrangements of normal streams. These streams often have fairly sparse aquatic vegetation and may suffer scouring floods from time to time, but they still represent excellent habitat and have abundant trout populations. Many people feel more at home on this type of stream than on a spring creek.

There are many streams that could be considered a bit schizophrenic, with many of the characteristics of both freestoners and limestoners. Often a stream originates up on a mountainside, with no limestone present, but flows down into a valley where a spring might give a stretch of the stream many limestone characteristics. In some cases there might be a large limestone spring followed by a relatively long stretch of flow in a nonlimestone area, creating a stream that has such freestone characteristics as classic pools, waterfalls, and heavy pocket water but also has the constant temperature and high fertility that typify a limestone stream. Since limestone is widespread and doesn't neatly follow watershed boundaries, it is logical that there are many degrees of limestone influence present in any particular stream. They vary widely. That is why it was necessary for me to visit each stream to check it out.

Limestone streams are intimately bound to the stone giving them their name. Limestone frequently has very substantial groundwater yields in wells or springs, whereas other rocks yield only a small fraction as much water. The relatively high solubility of limestone compared to other rock gives its groundwater the high alkalinity that is so important. Also, the soil produced by weathering limestone yields very rich lands, and the agricultural practices that the adjacent lands support will have a major influence on the stream. It is fair to say that the highly productive soils in limestone areas produce active land use.

Pennsylvania is blessed with substantial limestone deposits, which are widely spread throughout the Commonwealth. While there are a large number of gorgeous and justly famous spring creeks in the south-central part of the state, there are also quite a number scattered throughout the eastern and central parts, as well as outposts much farther north and west. In fact, many of these more remote streams are easier to fish and might hold larger populations of large fish than the popular ones in Cumberland County.

Approximately four hundred streams have been identified as having a limestone influence. This means that a stream might cross a limestone belt where it picks up a strong input of spring water, as in the case of the North Branch of the Mahantango Creek, or it might rise as a major spring in a limestone area but have most of the stretch of interest in a freestone area with the limestone characteristics continuing (such as Penns Creek or Antes Creek in Lycoming County). The streams might be classic limestone spring runs, such as Beck Creek in Lebanon County, or the Letort, or they might be rough pocket water like much of the Bushkill in Northampton County or the nearly vertical Roaring Run of Blair County. They might be tiny jewels, such as Franklin County's Willow Hill Spring Run, or major rivers, such as the Little Juniata. But they all have a number of things in common. To the extent of the limestone influence, the streams generally—but, puzzlingly, not always—will have rich habitats and substantial trout populations. If the habitat is right, some fish will be there, heavy fishing pressure or not.

A part of this project was to locate the limestone streams in the Commonwealth, but, in addition to finding far more limestone streams in Pennsylvania than I had originally thought, I also became aware of others scattered around the country and the world.

It is not surprising that the limestone beds in Pennsylvania continue down into Maryland and Virginia, across into New Jersey, and up into New York. Maybe the beds aren't as large, but the limestone and the streams it influences are there nevertheless.

Other parts of the country have substantial limestone areas, as well. Vermont's Battenkill might be considered a limestoner, since much of its valley is along a marble bed. Michigan's Au Sable similarly looks—and to a large extent acts—like a spring creek. Perhaps there is limestone below all that glacial till that does good things to the stream.

Spring creeks have turned up in such unlikely places as northern Maine, and rumor has it that some Nova Scotia salmon rivers are limestoners. Wisconsin and Iowa have classic spring creeks with massive trout populations to match. Missouri has true spring creeks with low gradients, lots of aquatic vegetation, and wild trout. Some of the Ozark streams have limestone influence as well. Even unlikely Nebraska has limestone water and spring creeks.

I once had the opportunity to spend a few days in southeastern Minnesota, where nearly a hundred lovely limestone streams are located. Many of these are true spring creeks, full of aquatic vegetation and wild browns. These are low-gradient streams, but in a country with considerable hillsides, very reminiscent of central Pennsylvania. In general I found the abundant browns to be on a serious diet. They were hugely unimpressed with my efforts. The more elusive brookies were on an absolute hunger strike. The fishing was better than the catching, but the plethora of fish made it clear I wasn't up to the needed standard. I did eventually figure things out to the point of convincing a number of nice browns to feed, among them a very heavy 10-incher with parr marks. There is plenty to eat in these rich streams.

Montana and Idaho have justly famous spring creeks rising from limestone strata. Alberta, Canada, has some classic limestone water, including the North Raven River, which is a spring creek. The mountains west of Calgary, in Alberta, are often pure limestone, which puts its stamp on their rivers' drainages, including the famous Bow River.

In many ways it all started on the limestone streams (locally called chalk) in England. Much of our fly-fishing tradition goes back to those hallowed waters. While they are clearly exceptional waters, the "take-no-prisoners" policy of killing all fish caught has affected the quality of the fishing. On a recent trip there, I stopped by the Test, which indeed is a marvelous body of water. The stream is split into numerous channels, so there are many "Tests" at any particular point. While much is club water, some small sections can be fished—for a price. One such piece is a section of three hundred yards on one bank of a channel just above the small town of Stockbridge. For about $100 per day an angler can try his luck for a few stocked fish. By comparison, our system looks awfully good.

France, particularly Normandy, also has many chalk streams. These are definitive spring creeks with seductive currents, lots of vegetation, and many fish. But here again the policy is to kill anything caught, often depleting the gene pool of wild fish. Adding stockers really doesn't make up the difference. I once spent a weekend on La Bresle, and turned up a few wild fish. They were similar to the British browns, generally with muted colors and little red showing, not the bright wild fish with butter yellow bellies, crimson spots, and adipose fins that we see here. The severe limitations as to what can and can't be fished—and the high cost—make our local conditions very attractive.

Spain has substantial limestone areas. On a visit to a limestone mountain range in the southeastern part of Spain, I saw a fairly exotic strain of wild browns with a myriad of tiny black spots—like many rainbows—and almost no red spots. The limestone waters were very productive; however, just about anything caught was killed, and rainbows were being used to restore fishing quality.

I'm told there are some glorious limestone waters in Yugoslavia. And a number of areas of Germany are underlain by limestone and have streams to prove it. I'll bet places farther afield also benefit from limestone geology.

The basics remain the same, though, no matter what part of the world you're in: limestone is highly permeable, so water yields are very large; the waters are rich in nutrients and maintain more nearly constant temperatures than freestone streams; and while not all limestone waters are spring creeks, the influence appears to be positive. It isn't always obvious where the trout come from, but they will be there—sometimes wild, sometimes stockers that have sought out these special waters to escape less-desirable conditions elsewhere. The bottom line is that, if the habitat is right, there will be trout, and limestone makes the habitat right.

WHAT'S IN A NAME?

My visits to the limestone streams across the Commonwealth gave me a very clear picture of how the original pioneers found their way west, and where they first settled when they got there. They were no fools. They understood that limestone meant good land and good water. Once the limestone valleys were all settled, other less-fortunate people tried and often failed to establish farms on adjacent lands with less-giving substrata. The shakeout from this process continues today. The limestone valleys are full of well-kept farms, while the next valley, with shale or sandstone substrate, has barns in a state of collapse and "For Sale" signs in overgrown fields.

Legend has it that when the first settlers headed west across Pennsylvania, they sought out stands of walnut trees as being indicative of good soil, while cedar indicated the opposite. Since it seemed logical to me that people would naturally gravitate to what they recognized as productive areas and avoid those that weren't, I thought that searching for streams with names like Walnut Run would bring me to good streams, while streams with names like Cedar Run would be the reverse. I found, however, there aren't many streams named Walnut Run. There's a Walnut Run in Lancaster County, which may be in an agricultural area that is too productive, as it is thoroughly blown out. And the Walnut Bottom Run in Cumberland County is thoroughly forgettable. So much for logic.

Cedar Run, however, is a very common name, and time after time streams of this name turned out to be outstanding fisheries. Cumberland, Centre, and Clinton counties all have a Cedar Run, and all are outstanding wild trout fisheries. Cedar Creek in Lehigh County is the same. And although Cedar Creek in Lancaster County appears troutless, it looks promising, far better than the neighboring streams in the much-abused Amish country. Only Cedar Spring in Juniata County does not live up to its more famous relatives.

Adding another twist to stream names, other fairly common and enticing names include Trout Run and Limestone Run. Chester, Berks, and Huntingdon counties all have a Trout Run, but they are basically wipeouts, with trout few or long gone. While Lehigh County's Trout Creek does have some lovely wild browns, the area around it sends shivers up my spine. The stream is more a triumph over environmental abuse than anything else.

Limestone Run and Limestone Creek certainly sound hopeful, but that's as far as it goes. There are streams with those names in Armstrong, Fayette, Northumberland, and Union counties that are totally blanked out. And Limekiln Run in Berks County and Limeville Run in Lancaster County are both terminally ill from man-made abuses.

Not surprisingly, Spring Creek (or Run) is also a frequent name, but there seems to be no pattern: in Centre and Franklin counties they are memorable streams; those in Berks and Fulton counties are nice, if modest, streams; while in Huntingdon and Adams counties the streams with that name are totally forgettable.

Nevertheless, I did discover that there are some marvelous streams out there with very colorful names: Snake Spring Valley Run, Oysterville Creek, Boiling Spring Run, Slab Cabin Run, Yellow Breeches Creek, Warriors Mark Run, and Standing Stone Creek are all names rich with images of events real or imagined. My favorite name is of an unfortunate trickle in Huntingdon County: what a marvelous name was given to Shy Beaver Creek!

PROBLEMS

The limestone influence almost always appears to be positive, and it would be great if every stream could cross limestone for a part of its course. But there is a down side to the limestone influence, and it may be seen most clearly in Lancaster County, site of the greatest concentration of limestoners in the Commonwealth. The problem is that the farming is *too* good. Farming practices sometimes take on aspects of dirt mining, and the streams suffer accordingly. There are few decent limestone streams left in Lancaster County as a result of the extremely intensive farming practices. This is changing, but slowly.

It is clear that land-use practices dictate the water quality of our streams. Chris Hunter in his book, *Better Trout Habitat* (which should be required reading for all TU leaders), sums up as follows: "Only the wise stewardship and management of the lands within the drainage will allow the long-term self-sustaining health of our streams and their trout populations." I dedicated this book to the landowners, since they will determine not only whether we have permission to fish their waters, but also whether those waters are worth fishing.

In my research certain themes cropped up repeatedly. One of the most obvious land-use variables concerns the interaction of cattle and streams. There is no question that farmers deserve all the help they can get. They work long hours for very low returns, their numbers are inexorably dwindling, and anyone advocating anything that will increase pressure on them is considered to be cold hearted or worse. Having said that, however, I also must say that, by and large, cattle have a devastating impact on streams, especially small streams. Their hooves tear out and ultimately flatten banks. Pools and riffles—the configuration that trout have evolved to live within—lose their natural shape and become wide, flat solar receptors. Many streams have thermal problems that can be traced directly to land-use practices involving concentrations of cattle along streams. And, not surprisingly, these large concentrations of cattle produce large quantities of waste products, which in many cases end up in the streams, either directly or by being washed off the adjacent land. This adds even more nutrients to streams that are already very rich, and sometimes the streams are simply overwhelmed. In several cases substantial fish-kills have resulted from poorly managed manure storage. A major Trout Unlimited initiative in central Pennsylvania involves working with farmers on manure management.

Anyone who doubts the impact of cattle on streams need only visit eastern Lancaster County; Spring, Rowe, or Church Hill Spring runs in Franklin County; or parts of Bachman Run in Lebanon County. These potentially great spring creeks have been heavily damaged, sometimes obliterated, by cattle along their banks.

One bittersweet commentary on the overlap of cattle and streams, however, is that it appears to be a diminishing problem at this point. Milking herds are fewer and smaller as the marvels of genes and scientific farming boost the output of each animal to previously unimaginable figures. Beef is viewed as less desirable now than some years ago. It is probable that fifty years from now the fishing will be better.

It is unfair to say the farmers are to blame and should be punished. Instead, we need to work out acceptable and attractive ways for them to keep their cattle out of streams. Government budgets are always tight, and easy solutions might not be possible.

Exclusionary fencing is one solution.

If we want to continue to eat beef and use dairy products, we will need sufficient numbers of cattle to provide these products. Quite naturally, the meadows where the cattle spend most of their time are on low ground that does not lend itself to cultivation. Is it then inevitable that there will continue to be the problem of cattle and trout streams? Not really. Exclusionary fencing—that is, fencing to keep cattle away from the stream—has proven effective again and again in protecting habitat and water quality. This solution involves obtaining landowner cooperation, which is often difficult, but progress is being made. The combined forces of the Pennsylvania Fish Commission, the Soil Conservation Service, and the Chesapeake Bay Foundation (for waters in that drainage—the great majority of Pennsylvania and its limestone streams), with the help of the Pennsylvania Game Commission, have been attacking the problem.

It is a slow process, but converts are being won as demonstration projects move ahead and skeptical neighbors see how well it works in their area. Money is available to defray most of the costs and publications are being distributed to point out the advantages to the landowner. This is an area where TU could be more actively involved.

In a few cases quarries appear to have damaged adjacent streams. Washing crushed stone can generate a lot of limestone fines which, though desirable in acid-rain-impacted areas, can smother life in less-acidic waters. It is silt, and like any other silt it should not be in a stream. In some cases the silty wash water is run through very effective settling ponds. However, the water in these ponds heats up and, if discharged, has a negative effect on the receiving stream. I noted a few cases where such warm wash water overwhelmed the stream, warming it well past tolerable limits for trout.

On the upbeat side, General Crushed Stone Company of Downingtown, Pennsylvania, worked closely with the nearby TU chapter to limit its stream discharges and to maximize wash-water recycling by keeping silt and warm water on its property. It is possible to work out such problems, but it takes persistence and goodwill all around.

Another recurring theme, and a dark one, is the impact of sewer plants—and poorly controlled effluents—on limestone streams. The main problem seems to be a basic one: these facilities are designed and operated with a very small margin for error, so errors often occur. While it is possible to design proper facilities and hire competent operators, we need a set of specifications more stringent than those currently used to monitor this type of facility.

The Chesapeake Bay Foundation made a study of sixty-nine sewer plants in Pennsylvania that discharged into waters ultimately feeding into the bay. This effort was a paper chase that involved examining records of monthly reports submitted to the DER by the sewer plant operators. Since these were monthly figures, instantaneous aberrations in effluent control could not be caught, although, of course, they could be lethal to stream life. Of the sixty-nine plants reviewed, fifty-nine showed violations in water-quality criteria during the year studied. In one case, one of the few plants apparently in compliance was found to be falsifying their records. No effort was made to go into the field and cross-check the reports.

An instantaneous malfunction can, of course, annihilate life in the receiving water. It's not good enough that the treatment plants run efficiently 99 percent of the time—try not breathing one hour out of a hundred. They must work well all the time. At present they simply are not equipped to do this.

A further problem involves the use of chlorine to kill any pathogens that have gotten through the earlier treatment system. There is no question chlorine is an effective disinfectant, and killing pathogens has led to major improvements in our public health. But trout are unbelievably sensitive to chlorine—even very small overdoses take a terrible toll. We know that ozone and ultraviolet light are effective alternatives. They cost a bit more, but they are safe. We are coming to realize that not only is chlorine lethal to trout, it can have some human health consequences as well. It isn't only pathogens that get chlorinated: a wide variety of organic chemicals in the water are also affected. Some of these remain in the streams and cause problems with the drinking water generated from facilities downstream.

Trout are like miners' canaries: if they aren't there, then something is wrong. In stream after stream the trout populations above the sewer plants were abundant and healthy, but below them, if trout existed at all, they had suffered. In no case was the fishing better, or even as good, below the point of discharge. These are casual observations only, not a definitive study, and there is clearly a danger of reading too much into small samples. Most reasonable people would conclude, however, that there is some connection between a sewer plant and a lack of trout below it.

Further confirmation of this is the story of the Letort. For many years a sewer plant well above the mouth of the stream was responsible for badly degraded conditions below its point of discharge. When this was moved, the trout population below that point thrived, giving several additional miles of very productive trout fishing.

Don Douple recalls other solutions. Quittapahilla Creek in Lebanon County was a thoroughly dead stream before the sewer plant was improved and the pollutants entering the stream were reduced. Quittapahilla Creek is now a healthy trout stream. Doubtless there are other success stories.

In the case of my own TU chapter (Valley Forge), we are dealing with the installation of a new sewer plant on our home stream, West Valley Creek, and we are pushing hard to have the plant installed with no stream discharge. We favor a widely proven plan for using the treated effluent on land, the way nature deals with the pathogens and nutrients that typify sewage. The plan involves extremely long treatment times—so momentary malfunctions are of little consequence—and returns the discharged water to the groundwater supply after natural biological processes remove every obnoxious component. Sewage then becomes an asset, and a much-loved stream is protected.

If one is a pessimist, one might say that limestone streams represent the trout streams of the future since their high-alkali content will neutralize the otherwise devastating impact of acid rain. Although the problem of acid rain is now being addressed by tighter laws and further research, it isn't clear if some freestone streams, with their low-alkali content, can be saved. The acid-rain impact is cumulative, and once the buffering capacity is exhausted, the stream is lost. With limestone streams this will not happen until the underlying limestone is also corroded away.

An even more severe threat to our world is global warming. While the jury is still out on how real this problem is, it is fair to say that limestone streams are better able to cope with it if this threat does turn out to be real. Groundwater, which is what springs discharge, stays at nearly constant temperature year-round. The constant temperature reflects the average temperature through the year for that location. In much of Pennsylvania the range is from 50 to 54 degrees Fahrenheit. If our climate warms up a few degrees, then the groundwater would also warm up a few degrees, say from 52 to 56 degrees. For limestone streams this would not be lethal, but for freestone streams, which are more easily harmed by the ambient temperature than the average year-round temperature, these few degrees would eliminate much of the trout habitat.

The greenhouse effect, if real, would mean a shift to the north for trout waters. There are famous limestone springs in many tropical areas where the average temperature is already too warm to support trout. Florida, for instance, has limestone springs that run warmer than the thermal limits for trout. Some limestone waters in the Midwest or the South would probably be lost if the average temperature rises a few degrees. To the extent that many limestone streams may not be pure spring creeks, but reflect a mixture of both freestone and limestone characteristics, many of these might be lost if global warming does occur. However, the limestone influence in those streams would be a positive factor.

Fishing limestone streams often means fishing in urban settings. The Letort, doubtless the most famous of them all, flows through the center of Carlisle. The Monocacy runs right through Bethlehem, while the Little Lehigh transects Allentown. Nearby Trout Creek and Nancy Run prove that good limestone streams can stand abuse and still produce wild trout. The Bushkill in Easton and the Logan Branch near State College show that having a factory on the stream bank does not spell death to the stream. It is not surprising that towns have sprung up on the banks of limestone streams, since the area would have rich agriculture, and sometimes industry, based on the soils or substrate of the area. That limestone streams continue to exist in the midst of heavily populated areas, if there is no sewer plant nearby, remains a marvel to me. Time after time I have asked myself, "What is a great stream like this doing in such a place?"

Not surprisingly, areas having very productive streams are full of other wildlife as well. Fishing the limestone streams brought me close to mink, deer, raccoons, wild turkeys, grouse, porcupines, a few bears, industrious beavers, and frenetic weasels. If there is one species I have gotten to know well, it's the wood duck. Endangered just a few decades ago, the wood duck has now multiplied beyond our wildest expectations. While I have great respect for this elegant creature, I do admit to wanting to get even during hunting season for the many times molted hens escape my intrusions by scampering at top speed upstream and terrifying all the trout. My efforts to circle above them always end up a few feet short, and they go splashing upstream, putting down fish in a few more pools. Wood ducks are a welcome addition to our world, but just sometimes I wish they would decide to run up on the bank and hide in the weeds.

Something else I noticed was the large number of carp that often populate cold-water streams. Doubtless they are there to stay, but they cannot be considered a positive influence. At first I thought it was odd to see them in cold water, but as I visited more and more streams and they kept showing up, I reached the conclusion that they had adapted as well as their fellow German immigrant, the brown trout.

Ironically, one of the problems in fishing limestone streams is that there is so much to eat it's often difficult to get the fish to pick your particular offering out of the plethora of available food. If you think about it, I guess that's not such a terrible problem!

An encouraging observation is that very few of the fine limestone waters of the state are posted club waters. The water is there to fish, and most of it, including the really great water, is available to the public. There are a few famous exceptions, with Spruce Creek in Huntingdon County doubtless being the prime example. In some areas it is wise, as well as courteous, to request the landowner's permission.

One of the joys that came with this research was to run across Trout Unlimited projects on various streams. Some of these projects involved building wing deflectors, as has our Valley Forge Chapter, and it was a pleasure to note the efforts of others. Blair County has done good work above the paper mill on Halter Creek. The Tulpehocken Chapter has launched the most massive effort in such work with huge wing deflectors erected below Blue Marsh Dam. This project narrows the stream and allows the discharged cold water to flow downstream and not immediately warm up and be wasted. An amazing urban fishery has resulted from their efforts. Havice Creek has structures built to deepen and narrow it. Donegal Spring Creek shows the results of many years of loving care, and it supports a good population of stockers through the summer and a few wild fish as well. These are the only wild trout I found in all the limestone streams I visited in Lancaster County.

The upper Letort has been squeezed by Cumberland Valley's efforts, producing deeper water and better holding areas. The Little Lehigh Chapter has done yeoman work protecting their lovely water from all sorts of threats caused by rapacious development. Falling Springs shows the attention of the local chapter, which has made quite an impact. And the Monocacy Chapter's monument is the stream itself. It's a marvel in the center of Bethlehem and in great shape because of their efforts.

Doubtless many other projects were missed or, perhaps even better, not recognized as such, since the best stream improvement quickly becomes invisible to all but the trout who take up residence.

Time after time, I would stop fishing and catch myself thinking, "This is a really great stream, why isn't someone taking care of it?" Therein lies the dilemma: how to handle the hidden gem. It is not my intention to expose these hidden marvels to hordes of people who might unwittingly spoil them. I admit wanting them to stay hidden. So why do a book announcing they exist? We are blessed with an abundance of marvelous streams, available to us for no more than the cost of our license. Their numbers are impressive, perhaps even overwhelming. And, in numbers there is strength. The sheer numbers of really good streams in effect become camouflage for each other and will naturally dispel the pressure concentrating on a few. At present there are tremendous pressures on a few justifiably famous streams in south-central Pennsylvania. However, many other streams as good or better exist elsewhere in the state and get nowhere near the attention they deserve. Nor the protection, and therein lies the rub.

"A stream without friends is a stream in trouble." This widely quoted statement, originally attributed to Lee Wulff, pretty well sums up why Trout Unlimited exists in the first place. There is a danger that a great little stream might be lost because no one is watching, because we are shoulder-to-shoulder waiting for the white-fly hatch on the Yellow Breeches rather than poking around in a much less famous, but perhaps far more satisfying, stream that does not get the headlines.

Of the four hundred or so streams discussed here, about one hundred are thorough wipeouts: they have been obliterated by cattle, they run underground in midsummer, or they have some other basic problem that will be tough to overcome. Another one hundred or so, however, are pretty good streams—a pleasure to fish and productive enough to generate a smile when recalled. A further one hundred and fifty or so are very good, with some special characteristics that have produced a memorable visit to a unique area and the chance to shake hands with a good wild trout population. That leaves about fifty that must be considered truly outstanding. I have not, deliberately, given each stream a rating—for instance, five stars for the best and zero for the worst. That would make the reader's job of identifying the very best much easier, but that's not the purpose of this project. I hope you will read through all of the descriptions in order to find those streams that might be worth including on the next trip to an area. Many of the streams are small; the number of large streams is pretty limited. If you insist on fishing only large streams, you'll miss out on some marvelous opportunities.

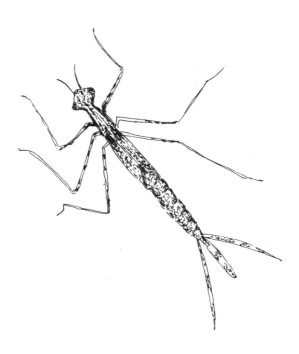

HATCHES

It must be said that Trout Unlimited is *not* a fly fishers' group. Thus, a section of this book devoted to hatches might seem inappropriate. When I asked Mark Nale about some hatches on streams in the central part of the state, he retorted, "Who cares?" Mark and his brothers, Frank, Paul, and John, catch more trout in a year than many dedicated trout fishermen catch in a lifetime (see Spruce Creek, Huntingdon County, for some of their comments). They do so with spinning equipment and a thorough understanding of what persuades trout to pounce on a well-presented lure.

Nevertheless, it also must be stated that many Trout Unlimited members are fly fishers of various degrees of skill (myself included), and we are interested in what might be hatching when we expect to be on a stream. So, since many TU members are fly fishers, some discussion about hatches will probably make this a more useful publication.

Why follow hatches? In practical terms, if there is a good hatch going on, generally the fish will be active and the fishing will be good, especially if a passable imitation of the hatching insect is presented in a manner that tricks the trout into taking the artificial. I certainly treasure memories of catching the green drake hatch on Penns Creek, or the sulphurs on Clover Creek in late May. Seeing all that teeming life, and the fish taking full advantage of the situation, is an experience to excite any fisherman. Such times can also be very humbling when things don't work out just right.

One of my all-time tragic fishing memories is the evening when I waded into position at a favorite place on Penns Creek and began to catch trout on my Green Drake imitation with almost casual ease. I would see a rise, I would cast, and I would be fast to a fish, just like that. As often happens if things are going too well, it's wise to look over a shoulder. During a cast I felt a little tick on my rod, like I had hit a twig or something. As I was out in the stream with no trees or twigs anywhere near me, it might have been a bat or bird. I'll never know, but although I caught the fish I was casting to, the tip of my beloved Paul Young rod suffered a green-twig fracture on that cast. There were another forty-five minutes of light, but my car and spare rod were forty-five minutes away, so all I could do was watch others enjoy the incredible activity.

Much of the fieldwork for this book was done in July and August, months not noted for impressive hatches (except perhaps the tiny but prolific *Tricorythodes*), so the major hatches were missed. However, fish were caught, and often the fishing was very good in spite of the lack of any substantial hatch. The fish are there all year and they have to feed, so they can be fooled into making a mistake. Since much of my fishing, by obstinate choice, is with an Ausable Wulff, which really doesn't look like any major hatching insect but which clearly looks very edible to trout, I tend to be less impressed with hatches than other people are.

At the end of this section there is a generic hatch calendar. This largely came from a well-known central Pennsylvania angler who wishes to remain anonymous. There are also substantial contributions from Bill Kodrich, former president of the Pennsylvania Council of Trout Unlimited. The hatch calendar doesn't apply to a particular stream but indicates what might be happening at a particular time of year. Since no stream has all these hatches, the listing should be viewed as being indicative rather than definitive. As is often the case, the emphasis is on mayflies. They float along the surface in stately form until their wings are sufficiently dried for them to take flight. They just plain look like something a trout ought to eat—and, of course, they do. Mayflies receive the majority of the love and affection of fly fishers. They are excellent indicators of water quality because, like trout, they require the best waters. Many of our classic fly patterns imitate various mayflies (including, more or less, the Ausable Wulff). Fishing mayfly imitations binds us to the long tradition of fly fishing, and one way or another seems to produce a sense of well-being.

Having said that, I'm going to throw a little cold water on things. In reality, day in and day out throughout the season, the caddis will probably produce more fish. Although they are prolific in some of the best quality waters in the country, caddisflies are more tolerant of less-than-pristine waters. And they often hatch in numbers rarely matched by mayflies. While it may be very satisfying to see a floating mayfly dun disappear to a slurping trout, it can be heart-stopping to see the slashing rise of a trout in hot pursuit of an emerging caddis. Splashy rises are a sure sign that it's time to put on a down-wing imitation or, better yet, a flymph or pupal imitation.

There seem to be zillions of different caddisflies, but they have not been studied as much as the mayflies. In general they are a good deal smaller than the classic mayflies, often size 16 or smaller. The drag-free drift so sought after with mayfly imitations can be totally unproductive with caddis. They don't follow the rules, but they do produce...and produce...and produce. One way or another, there always seems to be some sort of caddis activity on most streams. Often the trout key in on them, overlooking larger and seemingly more succulent mayflies that might be hatching at the same time. They might be sailing down the stream like a regatta, but if there are splashy rises, check to see what size and color caddis is coming off, as that is what the trout are concentrating on.

Stoneflies represent a distant third in the major aquatic insect orders of interest to limestone stream fishers. One reason is that stoneflies love heavy riffles and pocket water, which is rare on limestoners. Further, the stonefly's habit of crawling out on a rock to hatch, then flying from there, deprives the dry-fly fisher of most of his sport. Of course, some will fall into the water and make quite a rumpus until they either disappear or get airborne, but the long and short of it is that stoneflies are really not a major factor on limestone streams. When they are, nymphing is about the only way to get much mileage out of them. The good news is that stoneflies get to be very large, and swimming a large stonefly nymph through heavy pocket water can result in some spectacular fish pouncing on it. But that sort of fishing generally doesn't happen on limestoners. A few exceptions include the lowest part of the Letort and some stretches of Penns Creek below Poe Paddy, where heavy water creates ideal stonefly water and the fish know all about those large, succulent nymphs.

If there's a real odds-on hatch, which can be expected just about everywhere, it must be the sulphurs. These insects really put the "May" in mayfly. They are normally present in numbers that turn the fish on. Together with the Gray Fox, Light Cahill, and Pale Evening Dun, they represent nearly a month's worth of excellent fly fishing at a lovely time of year. It's too bad that this time can't be stored up and slowly released throughout the summer. So many streams, so little time.

After the sulphurs and other light-colored mayflies that hatch at about the same time, the next most prolific and widespread hatch is the *Tricorythodes*. It is tiny but it hatches in unbelievable profusion. It is really an experience to watch normally spooky fish lose themselves in gorging on the myriad floating spinners when they hit the water. The nice thing about the trikes is that they are predictable: every morning there will be clouds of them above the stream, especially in meadowside or open stretches. An old legend indicates they will hit the water when the air temperature hits 68 degrees. Some nights it never gets that cool, so this isn't totally true. But on hot, humid mornings they do their thing early, and by 9:00 a.m. the air above the stream is devoid of spinners. This generally brings out all the fish, which gorge themselves on the easy pickings. While I have never turned up a fish over 14 inches on trikes, I have seen larger fish grazing on the surface. And, while fishing a size 24 Trico is nowhere near as difficult as I had thought, I generally prefer to use an ant or a small beetle, which the fish seem to relish, and which are a bit easier to keep track of than the tiny trike spinners.

The other hatches mentioned will show up on some waters but not on others, so it is hit or miss. Also, the hatch calendar shown is basically aimed at upstate conditions. In the southeastern part of Pennsylvania things get going sooner—and in some instances much sooner. Blue-winged Olives, followed a week later by Blue Quills, generally get going in mid-March of most years (late February in an especially mild year recently) on Valley Creek in Chester County. I have seen heavy trike hatches as early as June 25 on Chester County streams. The farther north or west one goes, the later the hatches will occur.

Read the hatch chart and take the appropriate imitations with you when you go to the streams. But don't forget to bring along a mixed bag of caddisflies as well as terrestrials, which always seem to work. The most important thing is to watch. See what is going on, observe what is in the cobwebs, what is in the air. If swallows or martins are swooping over the stream, something is happening—see what it is. Keen observation will generally tell you what you need to know.

SMALL-STREAM HATCH EMERGENCE CHART

Imitation	Hatch It Copies	Date	Time of Day	Size
Little Black Stonefly	*Capnia vernalis*	March 1	Morning and afternoon	18
Little Blue-winged Olive Dun	*Baetis tricaudatus*	April 1 (two to three broods a year)	Morning and afternoon	20
Blue Quill	*Paraleptophlebia adoptiva*	April 12 to May 10	Afternoon	18
Grannom	*Brachycentrus*	April 15	Midday	10-14
Hendrickson	*Ephemerella subvaria*	April 20 to May 15	Early afternoon	12-14
Green Caddis	*Rhyacophila* species	May 1	Afternoon	12-16
Blue Dun	*Pseudocloeon* species	May 1 to June 15	Late afternoon	20
Sulphur Dun	*Ephemerella invaria* and *rotunda*	May 10 to June 30	Evening	16
March Brown	*Stenonema vicarium*	May 15 to June 10	Morning and afternoon	12

SMALL-STREAM HATCH EMERGENCE CHART (Cont.)

Imitation	Hatch It Copies	Date	Time of Day	Size
Gray Fox	*Stenonema fuscum*	May 15 to June 15	Afternoon and evening	14
Green Drake	*Ephemera guttulata*	May 18 to June 20	Evening (often in the afternoon on small streams)	10
Blue-winged Olive Dun	*Drunella cornuta*	May 20 to June 30	Sporadic late morning	14
Light Cahill	*Stenacron interpunctatum canadense*	May 25 to June 30	Afternoon and evening	14
Pale Evening Dun	*Ephemerella dorothea*	May 30 to July 15	Evening	18
Slate Drake	*Isonychia* species	May 30 to October	Morning	12-14
Cream Cahill	*Stenonema pulchellem* or *modestum*	June 15	Evening	12-14
Blue Quill	*Paraleptophlebia guttata*	June 15 to August 31	Morning	18
Cream Variant (Yellow Drake)	*Ephemera varia*	June 20 to July 25	Evening	12-14
Trico	*Tricorythodes atratus* or *stygiatus*	July 15 to September 15	Morning	24
Dark Slate Drake	*Hexagenia atrocaudata*	August 15 to August 31	Evening	8

WILD TROUT

Wild trout, as opposed to stocked trout, may be the ultimate goal of Trout Unlimited as an organization. This gets us into projects far afield from building in-stream structures or nurturing young trout for later release, but it is more important. Put in different words: habitat is where it's at. If we can protect or restore waters to the point where wild trout can reproduce generation after generation, we shall have accomplished a great deal. If there are trout in a stream, it says very good things about that stream. Similarly, if there aren't, something is missing, and the environment has been damaged. Since trout demand very clean, cool water, they seem to be on a collision course with "progress." That is why Trout Unlimited exists.

Many things have to be just right for trout to reproduce in a stream: lack of pollution, water in the right temperature range, proper holding water for each stage of life, suitable spawning gravel, food supplies, hiding cover, and a plethora of other finely balanced habitat requirements.

The neophyte fisherman probably doesn't much care whether the fish he catches are wild or stocked. A fish is a fish, right? Wrong! In the majority of cases the stocked fish simply do not have the skills needed to survive without the nurturing hand of man. In many cases the stocked fish have fins with frayed edges, or mere stubs of fins worn away against the concrete-lined pool where they were raised. Their color is often pale, and people with more developed palates than mine swear stocked trout don't taste as good as wild fish. Maybe so. Certainly, the stocked fish are not as wily, and catching them is generally not as difficult as catching a similar-sized wild fish. They are expensive and, frankly, not very satisfying.

A widely held myth is that wild trout are small and only stocked trout get to be an appreciable size. This simply isn't so. Admittedly, wild populations have relatively few very large trout, but they are there. And they are there in greater numbers than will ever be the case in stocked streams, except in those few cases where for various reasons a club might cram a small section of stream full of hatchery behemoths and then subject them to a fishing derby. This isn't fishing.

There are large wild fish out there, but, admittedly, they are hard to catch. Our society wants the instant gratification of catching stocked trout. Yes, the stockers do fill a need, providing fishing where otherwise there would be no opportunity to catch trout. However, the streams should be tested regularly to see if it is possible to establish a wild trout population.

If spawning clearly will not produce wild fish, maybe fingerling stocking will work. In a few cases planting eggs in proper places can produce sufficient numbers of stream-born fish to add spice to a population of stocked fish. But make no mistake about it, the wild product is superior in every way to the manufactured item. We need to protect those waters that are capable of producing wild trout and to work with those that currently are not but in time might be brought back.

Hatchery fish are needed to provide trout fishing in some areas where the streams cannot reasonably be expected to provide trout. Having said that, I need to say, as well, that many studies have shown that stocking hatchery trout on top of a viable wild trout population will mean fewer trout for anglers to fish over. On the face of it, this statement seems absurd, but as with many things that seem obvious, it is wrong to assume that putting more fish in a stream will improve fishing. Wild trout are territorial creatures: they have well-defined territories that they defend vigorously. The life of a wild trout, like any other wild creature, is an equation between intake of nutrition and expenditure of effort. If there is too much expenditure and not enough intake, the creature dies. Defending territory takes effort, but it does not directly produce intake. Hatchery trout are used to living in close proximity to others, so the tendency to defend a territory is not part of their upbringing. Put these gregarious creatures on top of wild trout and the social structure of the whole population breaks down. Effort is expended to defend territory that simply might be overwhelmed. Even if they are not fished over, a short time after stocking there will be fewer fish, stocked or wild, than there were before. Stocking is no instant cure for the ills of our streams. Ralph Abele, former executive director of the Pennsylvania Fish Commission, summed it up: "Politically attractive hatcheries are no substitute for improved water quality—in fact they are a dangerous diversion of effort."

CATCH AND RELEASE

"A trout is too valuable to be caught only once." This widely repeated saying could be attributed to the late Lee Wulff, who made many major contributions to trout conservation. It states the obvious: people fish to catch
fish, and if you want to catch more, you will have to take fewer. Catch-and-
release fishing was started several decades ago by a few individuals of vi-
sion who understood the tension between more fishermen and fewer fish.
By now it is widely embraced as one of the tools available to both the fisheries manager and the fisherman to make certain that more trout are available...and will remain available.

The beauty of the concept is that absolutely anyone can do it. The
neophyte might get a charge out of swaggering along a crowded opening-
day stream bank with a stringer laden down with fish, but the more con-
scientious, experienced fisherman realizes that, while a bit more subtle,
releasing those same (or often more) fish brings a deeper sense of satisfaction. It isn't necessary to show off the fish, since the satisfaction comes
from within.

There are some practical aspects of catch-and-release fishing as
well. If we fish primarily to obtain the limit, we then must shut down
for the rest of the day. By catching and releasing we can continue to fish
and to learn, and ultimately we will become better anglers. Frank Nale,
a spin fisherman who catches trout in numbers beyond our wildest imag-
ination, epitomizes catch and release. He was approaching five thousand
trout for the year 1990 in mid-September of that year! If he
had to stop at eight fish per day, he could never have put in the time to
learn the subtleties that have stretched his skills to their current outstanding levels. Admittedly, few people have the focus to reach this
point; however, the same truth applies: if the limit is reached and all fishing stops, many lessons will remain unlearned and much pleasure will
remain untapped.

Many studies have been done to check on mortality of released fish.
In general these studies indicate that fish caught with flies or spinners,
even treble-hooked models, have a mortality rate of around 2 to 5 percent,
while trout caught on live bait and released have a much higher mortality
rate, roughly 50 percent. It's clear that effective catch-and-release fishing
goes hand in hand with using artificials.

By releasing trout we can give something back to the resource that
gives us so much pleasure. I caught around fifteen hundred trout while do-

ing the fieldwork for this book. If I had killed all those fish, our streams would be that much poorer.

There is a further twist on catch and release. Many experienced anglers who decide to keep a few fish for dinner will impose some restrictions on what they are willing to kill. Often they release all fish larger than a certain size. Think about it. If you want to grow big cattle, large cattle are selected as breeding stock. Fast horses are used to breed even faster horses. According to an old Malay saying, a spotted cow gives a spotted calf. If you want to catch large trout, it makes no sense to remove them from the gene pool and return only the smallest ones. This skews the gene pool to produce only small fish. Release large fish. They have lived right to get to be that size and theirs are the genes that should be encouraged. Release some fish. It feels good and contributes to better fishing for all of us.

FISHING LIMESTONE STREAMS

Fishing the limestone spring creeks is forging a direct link to the early days of fly fishing, since the chalk streams of Hampshire, England, are nearly identical to our spring creeks. The English streams are steeped in tradition, as ours are starting to be.

This is generally tough fishing. The fish have seen it all and are not easily fooled. There is so much to eat that they have little incentive to make mistakes. In the more popular spring creeks the fish have generally been handled a time or two and, if equipped with the proper communication skills, they could conduct graduate courses in aquatic entomology. The flat currents can hide deceptively fast flows and make presentation a major problem, especially with subsurface fishing. Long, fine tippets are the norm, which can be frustrating when that once-a-season fish finally takes, only to dive into thick weeds. But sometimes things work out just right and the big one is played into submission, but hopefully not exhausted.

To a large extent limestone stream fishing is brown trout fishing. In an astounding number of cases these are wild fish, and they are agonizingly wary. While there are a few limestoners with wild brookies (Big Spring in Cumberland County pops into mind) as well as a few with wild rainbows (Silver Spring, also in Cumberland County), it is brown trout that have put down roots and generally become the dominant fish in these streams. Since there is plenty to eat, some grow to outrageous sizes.

Brown trout have the much-loved attribute of being quite willing to surface feed. Really large fish rarely will be taken while sipping minutiae off the surface, but their offspring do so with abandon and provide endless sport and frustration to fishermen. While other species of trout are generally viewed as being easier to sucker with imitations, I find that I catch more brown trout than other species since I fish with the sort of things they like (Ausable Wulffs), in places they like, and present in ways they like. I fish that way because I catch fish that way, and this means browns. And when hitting a new stream, generally I catch browns before I try any experiments.

The nearly constant water temperature of true limestone streams means that the fish are active, feeding hungrily year-round. There are midge hatches nearly all year, and there are often heavy mayfly hatches, especially the sulphurs of middle to late May. Tiny trikes can produce very fast fishing every morning from midsummer on, and terrestrials produce some of the most marvelous fishing of the season on summer afternoons. This can be exacting fishing to very unappreciative fish, and it is a triumph when everything clicks and a small dimple replaces a tiny ant or jassid. Although very fast fishing can accompany late-season flying ant hatches, they are the exception.

At the risk of offending purer and better limestone stream fishermen than myself, I must say that I enjoy fishing dry flies. It's easier than nymphing (two dimensions versus three—and far easier to see the take). For me that means fishing one pattern, an Ausable Wulff. I fish these up to size 8 and down to size 20. I often try different patterns, but I keep coming back to this one as the most productive for the widest variety of waters even though it is a heavy-water fly. Seeing those selective browns in the lakelike pools of Penns Creek slowly approach, study, and then softly suck down a size 8 during the height of the green drake hatch convinces me that something special is going on here. An Ausable Wulff has a reddish body and is an exceptionally poor imitation of a green drake. But they work, so I use them.

I use similar, although not identical, methods on the Letort and the Little Juniata, and I catch fish in both places (a lot more on the Little Juniata!).

When fish are sipping minutiae off the surface, there is no question that a light line and long leader will make an enormous difference in spring creeks. A 3-weight line will outfish a 6-weight line, so it makes sense to me to have appropriate tackle available for these demanding waters. The ability to make long, accurate casts is a great asset, but, regrettably, it is one that I have never acquired.

A careful approach is one of the least appreciated techniques for fishing tough fish. It means moving along a bank very slowly and staying low. It means wearing either outright camouflage clothing or what will functionally pass for it. And it probably means that the knees of your waders are the first place to spring a leak.

Since I'm a poor caster, I have to approach my quarry without spooking them. Patience is a real virtue in such efforts. While spooking fish in the heavily fished streams of the Cumberland Valley is not a big problem, a careless approach will make it infinitely tougher to convince them to take. In less-pressured streams such carelessness will send them fleeing in terror. "Gently, gently catch the monkey" applies to trout as well.

Many trout that are stalked in an approach from the bank might be more easily approached in the stream itself. You are lower when you are in the water, but you'll have to deal with other problems. Sloppy wading sets up small waves, which are sufficient warning to stop the most vigorous feeding frenzy. Move slowly, in slow motion, and work into casting position—unless it is very large water—no matter how poor a caster you might be.

A careful approach will allow you to make the all-important first cast a good one. I'm not saying that it isn't possible to catch a fish on the second or third cast if the first one is poorly executed. It's possible, but the odds are against you. Take time to work in as close as necessary to feel confident that your first cast will do just what you want it to do. Then, and only then, should you cast. This is what herons do for a living.

Matching the hatch is fun and generally productive, but there are many times when there is no hatch to match. The fish, however, have to eat, so the trick is to give them something they want. This mainly involves presenting something that looks good to eat in a nonthreatening way that makes it look like easy pickings for the opportunistic trout. For me this usually means floating my presentation above a likely lie or an actively working fish. This won't take all fish, especially the largest ones, which rarely surface feed anyway, but it will take considerable numbers of them and is equally true whether fishing dries, nymphs, or bucktails. If the presentation produces what appears to be an especially vulnerable meal for minimal effort or risk, it will be taken.

Nymphs can be drifted past the nose of a visible fish or in areas where currents converge. Generally, nymphs will do better if near or on the bottom, but I don't get much of a kick out of fishing that way. It is effective though.

If dries are the order of the day, there is no question that fishing over a frequently rising fish does get the adrenaline pumping. I think it was Ernie Schwiebert who wrote that if you see a fish rise twice, you should be able to catch it. Well, maybe that's true. He is certainly a better angler than I am. If I see a fish rise twice, I feel I have a sporting chance. It doesn't take very many seasons to experience the voraciously rising fish that totally ignores any offering except those from Mother Nature. On the other hand, fish that are visibly feeding do at least give encouragement.

Since limestone streams come in all sizes and descriptions, there is no magic formula that will always work—even the Ausable Wulff. A bit of watching will normally show where currents come together, and the subtle "X" on the surface will tell you that a fish should be there. The amazing thing is the extent to which those places do in fact hold fish.

Trout in limestone streams aren't all that different from trout anyplace else. They are spooky, if in a seldom-fished stream, or incredibly picky, if in a heavily fished stream. They have about the same holding patterns and act pretty much as other trout do. And methods that work on freestone streams work on limestone streams too. Persistence, a positive attitude, and some experimenting are what it takes to get them. The fish can be caught. They aren't easy, but they aren't impossible.

Enough of this, let's go out and visit the streams!

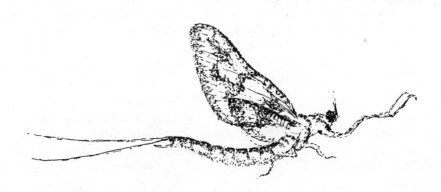

SOME NOTES ON PART ONE

The following were helpful to me in writing Part I: The Limestone. They appear in the order they are used in the book.

"Mineral Resource Report 50," *Atlas of Pennsylvania's Mineral Resources,* Commonwealth of Pennsylvania, Department of Environmental Resources, Bureau of Topographic and Geologic Survey, Arthur A. Socolow, State Geologist, Fourth Series, Harrisburg, Pennsylvania.

"Stream Map of Pennsylvania" by Howard William Higbee, published by the Pennsylvania State University, College of Agriculture, The Agricultural Experiment Station, University Park, Pennsylvania.

"Trout Fishing in Pennsylvania," Pennsylvania Fish Commission, Office of Information, Harrisburg, Pennsylvania.

"A Map of Pennsylvania Exhibiting not only the Improved parts of the Province but also its Extensive Frontiers, laid down from Actual Surveys and Chiefly from the late map of W. Scull published in 1770, and Humbly Inscribed to the Honourable Thomas Penn and Richard Penn Esquires, True and Absolute Proprietaries and Governors of the Province of Pennsylvania and the Territories Thereunto Belonging," printed for Robt. Sayer and J. Bennett, Map and Printseller, No. 53 in Fleet Street, London, published as the Act directs 10 June, 1775.

"Water Quality Standards," *Pennsylvania Code,* Vol. 25, Chapter 93, Department of Environmental Resources.

"Class A Wild Trout Waters," Pennsylvania Fish Commission, Bureau of Fisheries, Fisheries Management Division, Harrisburg, Pennsylvania, September 1989.

"Waters Proposed for Changes in Water Quality (DER) Designation," Fish Commission memo to DER, August 31, 1983.

"Acidic Deposition to Streams," Owen P. Bricker and Karen C. Rice, *Environmental Science and Technology,* Vol. 23, No. 4, 1989, p. 379.

Pennsylvania Atlas and Gazetteer, DeLorme Mapping Company, Freeport, Maine, 1987.

Better Trout Habitat, Christopher J. Hunter, Island Press, Washington, D.C., 1991.

PART TWO

THE STREAMS

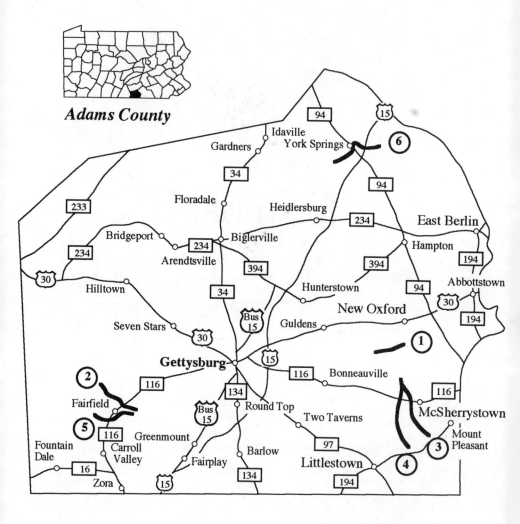

Adams County

ADAMS COUNTY

This pastoral county was the scene of one of the major events in American history—the Battle of Gettysburg. More than a hundred years later it all seems larger than life, a huge conflict that touched the lives of nearly every person and involved every corner of the county. Pickett's charge may have been the focus of much of the action, but the conflict was not restricted to the area around Gettysburg, as the historical markers dotted around the county indicate.

From the point of view of the trout fisherman interested in limestone waters, however, the history of the area is infinitely more alluring than the waters. If the weather makes fishing unreasonable in the better areas north or west of Adams County, it's well worth your time to poke around the battlefield.

Irishtown Run—1

I'm guessing at the name of this stream, which is just south of Irishtown. It has disastrous limestone influence, with loads of fines and silt from an adjacent quarry. It's a wipeout as far as trout are concerned.

Middle Creek—2

Just below Fairfield this nice stream is about 20 feet wide. It has good, cold water (60 degrees on a mid-June afternoon) and a bit of weed hinting at limestone influence. This stocked stream has clean gravel, but clearly cattle have degraded things. When I was there the holding water looked good, but I couldn't move a fish, perhaps due to the sparkling clear weather. It's a nice stream, no doubt better than it showed to me.

Larry Hartlaub of the Adams County Chapter of TU assures me that there is a good deal more to Middle Creek than my visit revealed. The chapter has a stream restoration project under way on the stream, and the stream is noted for its hatches of cahills, sulphurs, and caddis. In short, it has many limestone characteristics.

Plum Creek—3

This appears to be a warm-water fishery, and a forgettable one at that. There is no apparent limestone influence.

South Branch Conewago Creek—4

This substantial stream clearly has limestone influence. It is badly discolored, apparently with limestone fines from an adjacent quarry. At about 80 feet wide and generally slow moving with warm water, it is not trout water.

Spring Run—5

This nice little stream with the promising name is a feeder to Middle Creek. It's around 10 to 15 feet wide, but due to the presence of cattle often it is only inches deep. It is clearly a limestoner, with lots of weeds and cold water (60 degrees in mid-June). There is one enormous hole where a culvert under an abandoned railway dumps flood waters out below it. The hole appears to go halfway to Singapore and doubtless holds some big fish. The only trout I turned up, however, was a stocker rainbow with a taste for Ausable Wulffs.

York Springs—6

This little stream rises in a small limestone pocket. It has warm water and appears to be of no interest to trout fishermen.

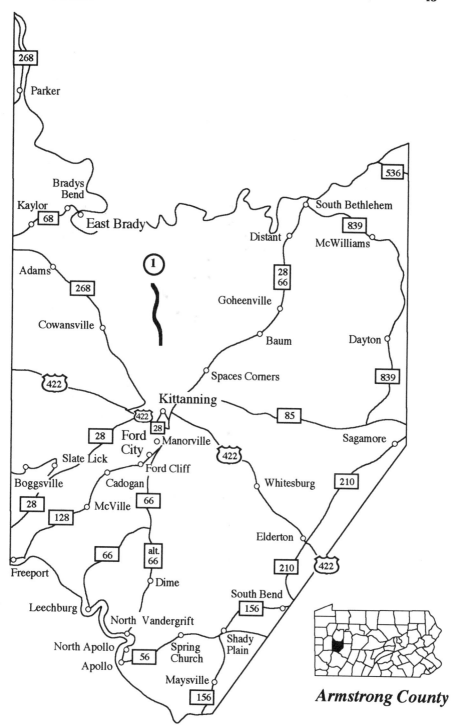

Armstrong County

ARMSTRONG COUNTY

Aside from having a marvelous name, this county has virtually nothing to offer in the way of limestone waters. There is a limestone deposit covering much of the county; however, it is too thin to have much impact on water quality.

Limestone Run—1

Limestone Run is a name that had to be checked out in an effort like this. I did so, and it can be forgotten. The stream is maybe 20 feet wide but lacks much good holding water. It has all the earmarks of a freestone stream, with ledges under hemlocks and rhododendron. The water is marginal at 72 degrees. No trout were in evidence when I was there.

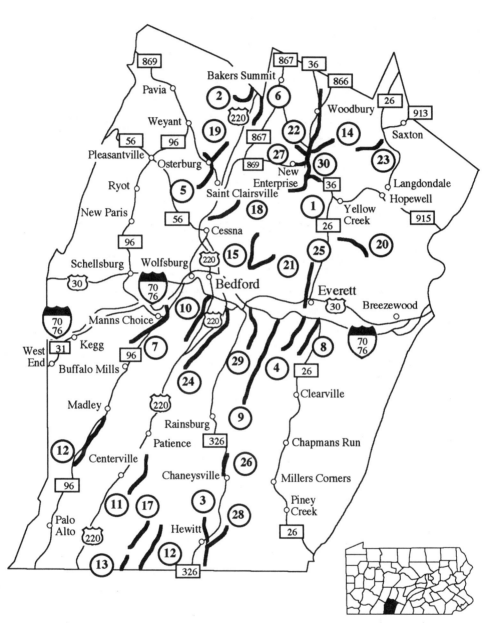

Bedford County

BEDFORD COUNTY

This is the westernmost outpost of classic limestone fishing in the Commonwealth. It is a large and varied county, with typical midstate ridge-and-valley topography, a few of those valleys in limestone belts. The parallel mountains give the area its appearance, but one valley may be wildly different from its neighbor. Some are based on red siltstones, which produce poor agricultural land (but some great deer and turkey hunting), while others are lush limestone valleys with classic limestone streams snaking along the bottoms. There is a large number of streams that pass over limestone at some point, but they seem relatively—or totally—unaffected by the brief contact, maintaining the appearance of freestone streams. There are lots of other streams, but with decreasing degrees of limestone influence.

One of the nice things about Bedford County streams, even the best ones, is that they are rarely crowded. This is not one of the obligatory stops on the limestone trail popularized by legend. Perhaps everyone knows that the really good limestone water is several counties farther east, so those who start in the east never get this far, while those coming from the west don't stop this soon. However, it is a beautiful county and well worth driving to, or stopping at sooner, depending on the origins of your trip.

Bedford Springs was the vacation haunt of presidents and remains a charming if somewhat anachronistic complex. Its combination of springs, each a bit different but generally all cold, forms Shobers Run and supports a good head of fish through the warm months of summer. Although some fish seem to be wild, most appear to be stockers. It's a unique area and fun to visit.

Beaver Creek—1

This stocked stream is a substantial feeder to Yellow Creek. I fished it a bit above Loysburg, which, I was told, is the best area. The only trout I turned up was a stocker, though. At that point the stream is about 25 feet wide, has nice holding water, pools, riffles, undercuts, and a considerable amount of weed in the slower parts. Paul Nale assures me this is curly leaf pondweed. Unfortunately, it also has a good crop of algae. Apparently there are temperature and silt problems as well, although I measured 58-degree water when I was there in early June.

Beaverdam Creek—2
See Blair County, Beaverdam Creek, page 69.

Black Valley Branch—3
This is a nice little stream, around 5 to 15 feet wide, with holding water at 65 degrees. It really appears to be a freestone stream, but it is a neat little piece of water. It also has loads of refugee trout. Although all the trout I handled or got a good look at appeared to be stockers, there might be some wild fish as well. There sure were a load of stockers!

Black Valley Creek—4
This stream is a true miniature, too small to be a trout fishery.

Bobs Creek—5
It could be argued that this isn't a limestoner since it doesn't flow over limestone—at least that I could identify. However, Osterburg Run does give it a jolt of cold water, which puts its imprint on the larger stream for some distance downstream. Bobs Creek is substantial, 30 to 50 feet wide, with some pools even larger. It has good holding water and tempting riffles. In general this stocked stream is rather neat looking. A beaver was quite at home in the best-looking pool, but it slapped its prodigious tail and put down all rising fish. There was a pretty decent hatch of size 16 tan caddis on the early October morning that I was there, and some splashy rising fish to match. In addition to what appeared to be a wild rainbow, I turned up a brown, but it might have been a stocker. This is really a nice stream, and while it gets pounded in early and midseason, some fish manage to survive. I'll bet some of the deeper holes have some very impressive fish.

Boiling Spring Run—6
See Blair County, Boiling Springs Run, page 69.

Buffalo Run—7
This tiny stream was 78 degrees and virtually dry in late June. Doubtless it dries up late in the season. It is not of interest to trout fishers.

Clear Creek—8

The limestone part of this stream is tiny and not of interest to trout fishers.

Cove Creek—9

This substantial, stocked creek is 30 or so feet wide below Kountzville. It appears to be a freestone stream and has some nice holding water, but with June water temperatures of 76 degrees, it clearly has thermal problems. The few trout I saw were holding on to a few spring seeps and were too busy staying cool to worry about food. I did get close enough to one of them to see that it was a stocker, which makes sense with this water temperature. Below Ottown the water is a bit cooler at 74 degrees, and up at Diehl Cove the water is around 72 degrees, so there have to be a few springs to cool things off. There are loads of rising chubs, and there must have been some trout somewhere, but the day I was there they appeared more interested in finding proper thermal conditions than in rising to my Ausable Wulffs. With enough time to spend, you could probably find trout by locating the springs, and some would most likely take. However, if the thermal problems were this serious in June when I was there, they must be a major concern in late summer.

Cumberland Valley Run—10

This tiny stream was virtually dry in late June when I was there and probably dries out completely in late summer. Not of interest to trout fishers.

Evitts Creek—11

This is a good stream! It is a totally different water, barely in the county, and quite unlike the others. It is really a freestone stream with a few limestone springs, but it has very pretty water, handsome pools and riffles, and pocket water. It's about 15 to 20 feet wide and has productive-looking undercuts where they should be. When I was there I found good numbers of what appeared to be stocker browns and rainbows, which gobbled my Ausable Wulffs. The fish seemed to be weathering midsummer (and the 67-degree water) in great shape, and one of the browns might just have been a wild fish. I didn't turn up any sublegals so I won't make any strong claims. Evitts Creek is a pretty stream and a pleasure to fish.

Flintstone Creek—12

This is a pretty freestone stream with little or no limestone influence. It is stocked and 15 to 20 feet wide, in general running warm (77-degree water when the midmorning air temperature was 74 degrees). After some poking around, I eventually came to a large, nonlimestone spring that had a pod of stocker brookies piled up below it. I managed to scare the wits out of them, and although they did mill around madly, they showed no interest in leaving the cooler water of the spring.

Gap Run—13

This tiny stream is really too small to be of interest to fisherfolk. In May it had 72-degree water, which is a good indication that it runs too warm later in the year. It is a tangle and doesn't have much to recommend it.

Hickory Bottom Creek—14

This is mainly a dry streambed, but there are a few places where it shows itself. A mile or so above the village of Waterside there is a bit of fishable water, if you like little streams. At Waterside there is an appreciable spring, but the stream is only a few hundred yards long from that point until its confluence with Yellow Creek. That short stretch is small and weedy and does not appear to be particularly attractive, but possibly there is a trout or two lurking in it.

Imlertown Run—15

This is a clone of Oppenheimer Run. It appears to be freestone—or rather free mud—and has nothing to recommend it. The stream is stocked, presumably to spread early season pressure. Don't bother in midseason.

Little Wills Creek—16

This small stream is shallow and probably dries out completely in midseason. The water is warm, and it just does not look like trout water—except possibly early in the season when it is stocked.

Lost Run—17

This tiny stream appears to be totally freestone. It is warm and just doesn't have much to recommend it. The most interesting thing I can say about it is that, on my way to it, I saw a bear going over the mountain, presumably to see what he could see. If he saw Lost Run, he would be disappointed.

Oppenheimer Run—18

This is a nothing creek. Maybe 6 to 10 feet wide, muddy (in dry weather), warm, and thoroughly uninviting. It has no appearance of limestone influence.

Osterburg Run—19

I managed to totally overlook this small limestoner, but a local resident mentioned it to me, so I made a return trip to the area and turned up some pleasurable small-stream fishing. Generally 6 to 10 feet wide, in the lower water (below Osterburg) it appears to be as deep as its width, while above it is shallower. But apparently it is totally signed off to a hatchery or nursery operation. The water is good and cold (in the mid-50s), and in open areas it has all the right weed showing. In summer the trikes are in the air, with sippers to pull them down. I didn't turn up a phenomenal number of fish, but I did get a nice wild brown and what appeared to be wild rainbows in two year classes. These might have escaped from the hatchery/nursery up near the spring head, but they were fine, fat fish, the way wild rainbows are supposed to look. If large streams are your thing, this isn't the place for you. But if you don't mind sneaking along tiny waters in search of a few wild fish, this stream is worth keeping in mind.

Pipers Run—20

This small stream—10 to 15 feet wide—doesn't seem to have much going for it. I was there during a hot spell in late May and the water was 72 degrees, which points to thermal problems later in the season. The stream is shallow for the most part and the water is murky, probably due to cattle upstream. There wasn't much good holding water and I was pretty discouraged. Then, coming around a corner, I saw a spot that practically shouted "trout." I flung out my Ausable Wulff, which was immediately engulfed by a nice brown. But that was the only fish I could entice that day. This is no great stream, but there are doubtless more trout than I turned up.

Pleasant Valley Run—21

The name is charming; the stream isn't. It's about 6 to 10 feet wide, freestone, warm, and muddy. It has nothing going for it except the name.

Potter Creek/West Branch Yellow Creek—22

This small stream is beautiful, about 15 to 30 feet wide, in a nice pastoral area. In the lowest part it has steep gradients, but higher up it is a meadow stream. It has clean gravel and nice holding water in the lower sections but shows some degree of abuse by cattle in upstream sections. It has wild browns and brookies, some of which get large enough to break off from a careless fisherman! In addition to the wild fish there are some state-stocked products as well.

Ravers Run—23

This stream is 5 to 10 feet wide and appears to have good holding water. The many stoneflies in evidence indicate good water quality. However, it was pretty warm (70 degrees) for such a small stream in late May. Although there is limestone in the area, I saw no obvious influence on Ravers Run. The only fish I could bring to hand were chubs, which usually means no substantial wild trout population exists.

Shobers Run—24

This is the stream flowing through Bedford Springs Spa. As such it picks up a lot of cold water at the spa, which is a glorious old health resort in the nineteenth-century style. Shobers Run is not a large stream, maybe up to 20 feet wide. Right below Bedford Springs it is cool enough (with water in the 70s) to have a respectable fishery, although it warms up as it goes downstream, thanks in part to the golf course, which allows a lot of solar heating. I turned up a number of fish, all of which were stocker-sized, although one of the browns appeared to be a wild fish. I also lost a sublegal brown, so there probably is some population of wild fish. There are a number of simply gorgeous springs feeding the stream, some with differing degrees of mineral content. The long and short of it is that the stream gets a real shot of limestone water in a short distance, and the fish are there in decent numbers.

Snake Spring Valley Run—25

What a great name! What an unfortunate stream! Cattle have obliterated it. Possibly sometime in the future, when cattle can be kept from mashing it, there might be a trout fishery here, but for now it is a wipeout.

Sweet Root Creek—26

A marvelous name and a charming stream. It's maybe 15 to 20 feet wide, and from just about everything I could see, it appears to be a freestone stream. It is classic upstate brook trout water, complete with the wild brookies and 64-degree water. There is nice holding water, which has been enhanced with some stream work. It's a lovely place to spend some time.

Three Springs Run—27

This pretty little frigid stream seems to have a fine population of wild trout and also receives some stockers from the state. I managed to lose those that willingly attacked my fly. I think they were brookies, but local information reveals that brookies are relatively rare compared to browns. There is a very well-preserved historic mill dam, and, in general, this stream has not received the heavy traffic from cattle that has degraded a number of other streams in the area. Paul Nale, who grew up nearby, called this stream "the best of the bunch." Strong talk considering the quality of the streams in the area.

Town Creek—28

This large stream is not really trout water. It is 40 to 50 feet wide but only about 6 inches deep above Hewitt, where I fished it. The bottom is shale and the stream is warm. Basically, it has poor-quality smallmouth water. There are stocked trout there, and when I was there in midsummer, I got into both browns and rainbows. They were crammed into the mouth of a feeder, stacked like cordwood, and some (which naturally I couldn't catch) were large fish. However, stocked—and stacked—trout don't inspire great trout fishing. When Paul Nale read this stream description, he noted that trout could be stocked into the lower Susquehanna in April and produce a trout fishery, but it would not be much of an experience. This stream might help to scatter opening-day pressure, but that is mainly what it has to recommend it.

Unnamed Creek—29

This stream with no apparent name is located between Shobers Run and Cove Creek. It could be a dear little stream except cattle have destroyed it. The water is cool enough, but there is just no holding water in its short length.

Yellow Creek—30

This substantial stream seems to have three or four personalities: heavy pocket water in the narrows below Loysburg, fine meadow fishing for sipping wild browns above, and tremendous frustrations in what appears to be lovely water above Little Pine Lake, where the wild trout water was overrun with an enormous run of spawning carp. There is a substantial population of wild browns, but it is also stocked. Frustrations aside, this is one of the major limestone fisheries in the state.

It is a good-sized stream, about 40 or 50 feet wide around Loysburg, which is the lower end of the limestone area. A number of lovely, small, frigid limestone streams keep Yellow Creek well supplied with nutrient-rich cold water, as well as wild trout, which may wander downstream to enjoy the added roominess of the larger water. These small streams can be delightful for those who like tight waters with lots of wild fish, both brook and brown trout. The springs keep the water temperature in the upper 60s or low 70s through summer.

On Memorial Day there were what I took to be March browns in the air. The pocket water below Loysburg showed loads of stonefly shucks clinging to some of the boulders. According to Charlie Meck, this is one of the few streams in the Commonwealth to enjoy an August hatch of white flies. Sections of the stream are classic spring creek water, where terrestrials can bring up shy sippers. I caught fish by a variety of methods, with the great majority of them being wild browns. I did not make it to the special-regulations area, which is downstream out of the limestone area. It would have to be pretty good to beat the parts I visited, with the major exception of "Carp Creek" above Little Pine Lake—at least in late May. This is a stream to go back to and spend a lot of time on.

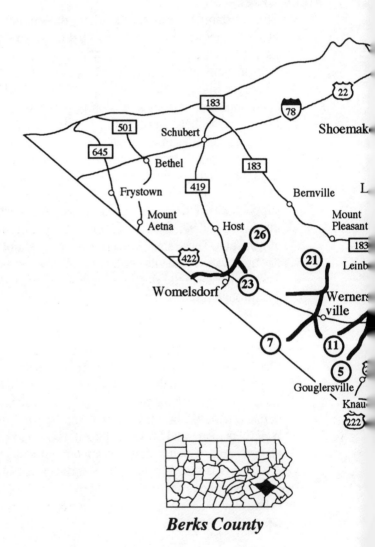

Berks County

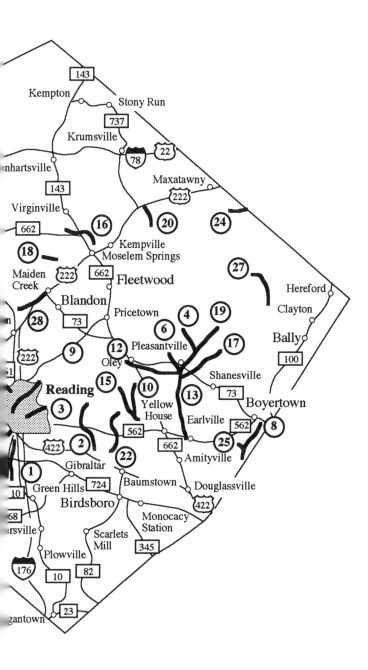

BERKS COUNTY

Fortunate are the people living in Berks County! They have a great tailwater fishery in the limestone Tulpehocken Creek, essentially in the midst of Reading, as well as a number of other smaller, but still fine, limestone waters available to them.

Some of the headwaters of the Manatawny Creek are limestone and have good populations of wild fish. Pine, Bieber, and Oysterville creeks all appear to be freestone streams, but with varying degrees of limestone influence and with varying wild brown trout populations. The Manatawny itself is a large stream but warms up in summer so is of less interest.

Another classic limestone stream is Mill Creek, or Wyomissing Creek, which flows through the center of Wyomissing, virtually a part of Reading. There are numerous large limestone springs, deep pools, lovely riffles, and fat browns. Willow Run, just north of Reading, is another limestone water, which, however, has been damaged by development. But with luck and a lot of hard work it might be saved and brought back as a premier fishery.

Other good limestone waters a bit north of Reading include Peters Creek and Moselem Springs Creek. Peters Creek was largely inundated by the Ontelaunee impoundment, leaving maybe three-quarters of a mile of stream. That stream, however, is full of wild brookies, a real rarity for public land in a fairly populated area. Moselem Springs Creek is rural, almost lonely, but is epic limestone water and has a thriving population of what appear to be wild rainbows.

Spring Creek, west of Reading, features an enormous limestone spring that turns the upstream freestone Furnace Run into a much larger and more productive fishery. Admittedly, I was somewhat put off by catching a carp on a dry fly here, but still it is a pretty piece of water. There are a number of other streams with limestone influence that would more accurately be called freestone streams. These are scattered throughout the county and offer worthwhile fishing.

Finally there are a fair number of "what might have been" streams—potentially fine waters that have been lost to the machinations of mankind. Limekiln Creek is a gorgeous little stream, but it has terminal thermal problems. Bernhart Run has nearly its total course inside culverts. It may have good temperatures, and possibly even quality water, but fishing in culverts is a real problem. Several other streams have been destroyed by the heavy hand of man, but they might be brought back if the effort were made.

Angelica Creek—1

This is sort of a junior varsity version of Mill Creek, which parallels it nearby. It has nice holding water, cool temperatures, and a nice size at 20 to 30 feet wide. What it doesn't seem to have is trout, which surprised me. It looks fine, and, in spite of its basically urban setting near Reading, it has a lot going for it.

Antietam Creek—2

Every history buff knows that Antietam Creek flows through Maryland and that one of the bloodiest battles of the Civil War took place on its banks. That's true, but there is another stream of the same name in Pennsylvania, in Berks County. This stream appears mainly to be a freestone stream, but it has elodea in it, and cool enough water that it appears to have some limestone influence. It's not a memorable stream, but it does hold a good head of stocked trout through the summer. In late August, when I was there, I managed to catch two stocker browns and scared the dickens out of a few others, but there was no evidence of any wild fish.

Bernhart Run—3

This urban stream flows through, and mainly under, Reading. The majority of its length is in culverts. There may be trout in it, but I couldn't reach down to them.

Bieber Creek—4

This nice stream is one of the major headwaters of Manatawny Creek. The uppermost part of this stream is freestone, but the lower section is limestone. It is maybe 20 to 30 feet wide in the lower sections, with good clean gravel, nice deep pools, some undercut banks, and logs in enticing places. The water isn't frigid, but, at 73 degrees, it's cool enough to hold trout through the summer. I didn't see a trout, which surprised me, as the habitat looked really good. Nearby sister streams, Pine Creek and Oysterville Creek, both have wild browns so no doubt this stream does too. I just wasn't up to extracting them. Cobwebs showed that there is a substantial trike hatch in the summer, and that may be the best way to run a population survey. I ran into some other fishermen who were principally interested in smallmouths, which they said occurred in sufficient numbers to make the fishing worthwhile, but one said he had recently caught a decent trout in the stream. It seems reasonable, although all I turned up were chubs—loads of them.

Cacoosing Creek—5

This is a fine-looking little limestone spring creek, maybe 15 to 20 feet wide, with lots of weeds and nice cool water (65 degrees in late July). An old jack dam is evidence of someone's effort at creating suitable habitat for trout, although there is good holding water in other places nearby. But there are no trout. The stream has been sacrificed to "progress," and could be a case study in abuse of a fine resource. Two sewage treatment plants overwhelm the lower stretches of the stream, although apparently there is some form of stocking done by some group. However, the fish were long gone by late July. The upper water fares no better as a landfill apparently drains into this section. This is a shame and begs for corrective action.

Furnace Creek—6

Just above Furnace Creek's confluence with the Little Manatawny there is reasonable water temperature (69 degrees) and decent width (10 to 15 feet). There's some aquatic weed, but the stream appears to be freestone. I only turned up chubs; however, I have a hunch that there are probably a few trout there. It's worth a shot if you're in the area.

Local feedback indicates that a landfill in the upper stretches contributes silt and leachate, that unspeakably filthy liquid that comes from rainwater percolating down through the trash in the landfill. Although this stream appears to be in trouble, it's worth some attention. Nevertheless, in Berks County there are so many other better streams that it is hard to figure who might have the time to stay on top of this one.

Hospital Creek, Manor Creek—7

These two small streams combine and flow into Spring Creek. This combination has a major thermal problem; however, it is a tremendous carp fishery, and if that's what turns you on, then this is your stream!

Ironstone Creek—8

A decent-sized stream, 15 to 30 feet wide, but basically shallow, it is to all appearances a freestone stream. There's not much in the way of decent holding water, but what there is has a good head of large chubs. While they might give good practice to budding fly fishermen, the fishing leaves something to be desired if wild trout are the quarry. This is a forgettable stream.

Laurel Run—9

This small, heavily urbanized stream just above Reading had 79-degree water the day I visited, which wasn't a particularly warm day, so it appears doubtful that there are any trout here.

Limekiln Creek—10

What a promising name. What a handsome-looking stream— small, only about 10 feet wide, with a good growth of aquatic vegetation swishing in slow, rich currents. Unfortunately, it is all in vain. The water is warm, apparently solar heated in a quarry-effluent settling pond. Mark up another stream lost to man's intervention.

Little Cacoosing Creek—11

This small brother of Cacoosing Creek has been spared the degradation of landfill and sewer plants that have wiped out big brother. It is a limestone spring creek, has lots of the right aquatic vegetation, is around 15 feet wide, and has good cold water (65 degrees in mid-July). But it doesn't have trout, at least in any noticeable numbers. Silt from agricultural mismanagement is the culprit. Fortunately, the situation is reversible, and in time, as more enlightened land-use practices spread, this could be a delightful stream. What a tragedy to waste such waters.

Little Manatawny Creek—12

On June 3, just above the confluence with Furnace Run, the air was 70 degrees and the water was 79 degrees, which told me all I needed to know. No trout!

Manatawny Creek—13

This substantial stream flows through the fascinating pastoral area just east of Oley, where a whole township has been declared a historic district. The stream is large, 50 to 70 feet wide, and gets inundated by stocked trout, followed by those interested in such critters. It really appears to be smallmouth water, although in late June I did manage to turn up one stocker brown, which was looking a bit harried by rising water temperatures (72 degrees). Sulphurs, *Isonychia*, stoneflies in the fast water, and various caddis were in evidence, but this really is not great trout water.

Mill Creek/Wyomissing Creek—14

In essence this is an urban stream. It runs through a park in suburban Reading where a few old farmsteads remain, each with a prolific springhouse. In the park there are a number of very substantial limestone springs that turn a freestone stream into a respectable limestoner. Stocked, Mill Creek is about 20 feet wide and has nice holding water, with very favorable temperatures. In places there are ledges with what amounts to pocket water. In others there are meanders with deep pools and undercut banks. It is a very pretty stream, especially for the urban park setting. The only trout I turned up was a stocker, but it was about the prettiest stocker I've ever caught. It appeared to be a holdover of about 13 inches and was starting to get wild fish coloration, including red-tipped fins. I know if I had invested more time, I could have turned up more fish. If this lovely stream were in a somewhat more favorable location, it probably would be famous.

Unfortunately, I later learned the stretch below Route 222, where I was fishing, is restricted to local residents. No signs were posted to this effect, but be forewarned. The stream is stocked above Route 222, while the lower water apparently has an increasing population of wild browns.

Monocacy Creek—15

A twin to Limekiln Creek, except it is larger, has less weed, runs marginally cooler, and is less attractive. It also appears to have no more trout.

Moselem Springs Creek—16

This is another "unknown" Berks County spring creek. It has one major problem: a golf course in dire need of water traps so the upper stream is dammed and the spring water warms to the mid-60s. Below, however, is a relatively brushy area that doesn't get much business. The stocked stream is about 30 feet or so wide, of low gradient, with all the right weed for a limestoner. It also has a limestone stream curse—enormous carp—but there are also trout. The browns I caught probably were stockers, but one might well have been a wild fish. The rainbows I turned up certainly looked like wild ones. The different year classes were distinct, and all had the appearance of wild fish. The fish were not easy, but they were possible. I looked for sippers and usually could convince them to take. It is a nice stream. It could be phenomenal if the golf course tried multiflora rose traps instead of water traps and let the springs give all their cold water to the stream.

Oysterville Creek—17

This is a medium-sized stream, maybe 15 to 20 feet wide, with some good clean gravel and cobbled-bottom areas. Unfortunately, 76-degree water on a hot afternoon flashes a warning light. A local sportsmen's club raises fish and runs one of those few-holds-barred fishing rodeos on the stream. They have carefully created a series of pools to hold their unfortunates during their brief sojourn in the stream. Why such streams have to suffer getting crammed full of "trophies" is beyond my understanding. The stream also has wild browns—not a huge population, but enough to make it fun to look for more. The stream is nice and worth poking around in. However, a word to the wise: local rumor says that the area is stiff with copperheads. I didn't see any, but such rumors need to be passed along for whatever they are worth. It's a shame that the copperheads don't participate in the rodeo.

Peters Creek—18

This small stream (maybe 15 feet wide at maximum but normally half that) has a number of strikes against it. The lower half was flooded by Ontelaunee Lake, and the upper half has been compressed between rock walls so it is sort of a channelized drainage ditch. Nevertheless, it is a tempting limestone spring creek. Although it is only about three-quarters of a mile long and was ditched by the Civilian Conservation Corps about sixty years ago, it is still a nice little stream. It has all the right weed and 54-degree water. Where the rock walls permit some overhanging cover, or the weeds break just right, there are lots of wild brook trout, more than what is needed to make it Class A wild trout water. What it could be if habitat improvement were done boggles the mind, as the CCC efforts really did the stream no favors. It is all in a heavily populated area on public land. The Fish Commission is scrambling to get special regulations in place, as this resource is too important not to receive protection. It is tough fishing, as even crawling on all fours does not permit one to get low enough. A long rod would be a godsend. However, the fish are here, and if none are huge, the numbers make up for it. This stream will become well known in the future for the powerhouse it is.

Pine Creek—19

Where I was, a bit below Lobachsville, Pine Creek looked like a nice trout stream: about 20 feet wide or so, with nice holding water, an impressive numbers of sulphurs in the air, and adequate 67-degree water. I could not turn up any trout, however. I am told there are wild browns upstream out of the limestone area, but I cannot confirm the report.

Sacony Creek—20

One stream, four personalities may be the best description for this creek. The headwaters are freestone; they have a healthy population of wild browns and some enticing water surrounded by "No Trespassing" signs.

Farther downstream the creek hits the limestone belt and prosperous-looking Amish farms, but here the quality is radically different. Although the water is stocked, it appears mainly to be aimed at spreading out opening-day pressures. When I was there in mid-June it was a warm, sluggish carp heaven. Since I was well into the limestone area, I figured that the rest of the stream was history.

Poring through the DER rule-making section in the Pennsylvania Bulletin one day, however, I noticed that a part of the lower Sacony has been proposed to be upgraded to a cold-water fishery. I went back up, and sure enough there was a good deal more to the story. Just above Kutztown, a substantial spring pumps cold, nutrient-rich water into the stream, and Sacony becomes a classic limestone spring creek, complete with swishing aquatic vegetation, water in the low 60s, and subtly sipping wild brown trout. Since this stretch runs primarily through Kutztown, the aesthetics, as with all urban settings, may be a bit lean.

The fourth personality of Sacony Creek is the least appealing. Just below Kutztown is a sewer plant, which puts the cap on any further trout fishing. The water looks good, if not overly lime-stoney, but it is full of chubs.

Spring Creek I—21

This stream is a combination of Furnace Creek (just downstream from Route 422) and a large spring there, which merge to become Spring Creek. Furnace Creek is stocked, as is the lower portion of Spring Creek. I fished between these two areas. It is absolutely stiff with carp. This is the only place I have ever caught a carp on a dry fly (an Ausable Wulff, naturally). Although rumor has it that there are wild trout here, I never turned them up. I did get a few stocker brookies, always a welcome fish in this part of the state. The stream is probably better than what I got out of it, but it is not the Shangri-la I had hoped it would be.

Spring Creek II—22

This Spring Creek is located east of Reading and should not be confused with the stream of the same name west of town. It does not appear to be a limestone stream. It is tiny, has very low water, and doesn't look capable of holding trout. When I was there in late August the water was warm, though the day was not particularly hot. This is one stream you can pass by.

Spring Run—23

This small limestoner just above Charming Forge would appear to be a classic in miniature, running about 6 to 10 feet wide with the right aquatic vegetation and cold water (lower 60s in mid-summer). What it needs are trout. No sign of them.

Toad Creek—24

This is one of the few feeders to the Little Lehigh that isn't worth a second glance. It is warm, sluggish, and the antithesis of a lime-stone stream. Don't bother.

Trout Run—25

This small feeder to Ironstone Creek (10 to 15 feet wide) has pretty decent holding water, including an enormous hole under an old railroad line. It also has lots of greedy chubs. Where there are a lot of chubs there generally aren't many trout, and that was the story here. The water was quite chilly: 66 degrees in mid-July. One fish I tangled with might have been a wild brown (there was a flash of yellow before it engineered a long release), but all the fish I brought to hand were chubs. It looks like a freestone stream, but with that cold water there probably is limestone influence.

Tulpehocken Creek—26

Although this stream is a true limestoner in Lebanon County, things get a bit more confused downstream in Berks County.

Above Blue Marsh Dam, Tulpehocken wanders in and out of limestone areas but does not exhibit many characteristics of limestone water. In large part this is due to a nineteenth-century water project, which turned much of the stream into a navigable canal. This may briefly have been good for commerce, but it left much of the stream a slow-moving, mud-bottomed slough.

Below Blue Marsh Dam the bedrock is metamorphic. Nevertheless, the water runs cold due to releases from the bottom strata of the impoundment and has a high pH, probably because of the considerable limestone areas of the watershed.

This is large water, well over 100 feet wide in most places, with slow riffles and an amazingly even bottom, which makes for easy wading. The fingerlings released by the Fish Commission in this tailwater grow with astonishing speed, matching growth in a number of the premier fisheries in the country. Though most of the insects are very small or infinitesimal, there are plenty of them. A size 54 caddis would be ideal if such a thing existed. This burgeoning insect life produces a bumper crop of free-rising, picky fish, both browns and rainbows, that look wild. These are fine, fat fish that fight like demons.

The tailwater fishery is in an urban setting quite close to Reading, so there are always plenty of fishermen on hand. A light-colored caddis size 18 or smaller is a pretty good bet, as is an 8X tippet. This stream is a major feather in the cap of the Fish Commission, as well as living proof of what a TU chapter can accomplish. The Tulpehocken Chapter participated in each step of turning this once overlooked and abused water into a marvelous fishery. They raised money to build what have to be the largest fisheries-improvement structures in the Commonwealth, and possibly the world: large deflectors constricting the stream so its precious cold water won't be heated and wasted in midsummer.

The Tulpehocken Chapter has also worked out the hatch calendar that follows. Although there are a few other insects of some interest (most notably the *Tricorythodes* of midsummer mornings), the caddis are clearly the main ingredient of fishing this stream. A final tip: wait until late in the evening, because some of those infuriatingly selective fish are more likely to make a mistake then.

TULPEHOCKEN CADDIS CHART

Body		Wing			Hook
Color	Size	Color	Size	Date	Size
Olive (Apple Green)	10mm	Brownish Dun	12mm	mid-April to May	14 & 16
Olive (Apple Green) or Green	6-7 mm	Brownish Dun	9-10mm	mid-April to October	16 & 18
Olive (Apple Green)	5mm	Dun	8mm	July to September	18 & 20
Tan	7-9mm	Brownish Dun	10-12mm	mid-April to July	16 & 18
Brownish Gray	10-12mm	Brownish Dun	14-15mm	late April to June	14 & 16
Black	12.5mm	Black	15mm	May	12 & 14
Dark Gray	7mm	Black	9-10mm	late May to June	16 & 18
Black	5mm	Black	8mm	July	18 & 20

Don Douple read over the above description and clued me in on other insect hatches besides the caddis going on in the Tulpehocken. His additions are below.

What	When	Size
Early Dark Stonefly	late January to early March	18, with some as large as 12
Ephemerella rotunda (called "Light Hendrickson" by many locals)	May	14
Ephemerella invaria	May	16
Gray Fox	May	12
Assorted Light Cahill types	June	12-18
White Fly	August	14

In particular, Don said the *Ephemerella rotunda* hatches are the heaviest he has seen anywhere. He also swears the white fly is there, which would be a major discovery if present in numbers great enough to excite the fish.

West Branch Perkiomen Creek—27

Near the village of Huffs Church there is a relatively short, isolated stretch of this stream underlain by limestone where it gets some cold, mineral-laden water. The stream is maybe 12 to 20 feet wide and has some nice holding water. Below Huffs Church there is some pocket water that verges on waterfalls. There are wild browns, mostly small, that have the same bland coloration as those in neighboring streams. Whether the condition of this stream reflects some effort by a Johnny Appleseed type or has to do with the underlying bedrock isn't clear. The fish are there. If this isn't a major stream, at least it represents yet another nice wild trout stream.

Willow Run—28

This small, urban stream is a limestone spring run generally about 15 feet wide with some wider places. It has been channelized in a few areas but runs cold: the water temperature was 64 degrees when I visited it in late August. A variety of aquatic weeds, overhanging grass banks, and other general features of a meadow limestone stream characterize Willow Run. But there was not much good holding water, and ducks seemed to inhabit much of the best water. The only fish I turned up was a sublegal brookie with gorgeous color. Though the stream could use some help, this is one of those little jewels that is worth fighting for. Urbanization is certainly an obstacle, but the Little Lehigh and the Bushkill have been able to cope with the pressures, so there is no reason why this fine little stream couldn't be turned into the marvelous fishery it shows the potential of becoming.

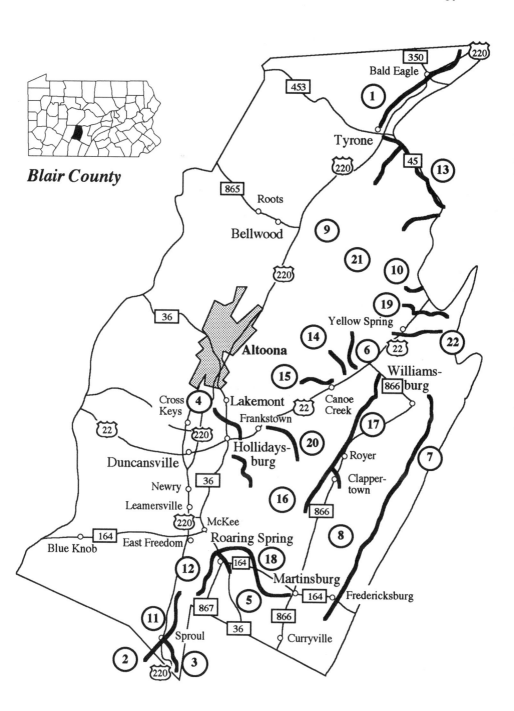

Blair County

BLAIR COUNTY

On the western boundary of the major Pennsylvania limestone areas, Blair County offers rich farmlands and some lovely limestone streams, many with good populations of wild trout.

Paul Nale, a member of the Blair County Chapter of TU as well as a former executive director of the Pennsylvania Council, says, "If the ditch is running in July in Blair County, it's a trout stream."

Clover Creek, and sister stream Piney Creek, must rank at the top of any list of limestone waters in Blair County. Both streams have great wild trout populations and also offer lovely settings in which to chase them. I have never found either stream particularly giving of its fish, but if I can see them and not catch them, it's hard to blame the water.

The Little Juniata, shared with Huntingdon County, is a justly famous large body of water. It has prolific hatches and great numbers of trout, some wild, some that grow up from fingerling stockers. It is great fishing, but the water is large enough to intimidate me, partly because I have never taken the time to get to know it well.

There are a few small, more or less vertical, limestoners with good wild trout populations, perhaps best typified by the very accurately named Roaring Run. These are small streams and require a certain point of view to be fished with pleasure. However, the fish are there, and they will cooperate if they haven't been spooked by a clumsy approach.

There are some distressing losses. Lovely Plum Creek is typical: it has all those "Jack Daniels" limestone springs pumping in cold water but cannot overcome a chronically malfunctioning sewer plant upstream and abuse from heavy concentrations of cattle. If those can be brought under control, this will be a marvelous stream—a project waiting!

There are also some heartening wins, including Halter Creek, which is a Trout Unlimited success story. The Blair Chapter eventually won the confidence of a large former polluter, changes were made, and a great little stream was reborn.

Blair County is classic upstate Pennsylvania limestone fishing. It has no true spring creeks, but heavy limestone influence has created some great fishing in beautiful surroundings.

Bald Eagle Creek—1

A limestone seam follows along this stream valley. The stocked stream is maybe 15 to 30 feet wide, shallow with very little good holding water. The water was cool but so was the air the day I was there, so it's hard to say much on that account. From all visible signs this is a freestone stream. No trout were in evidence.

Beaverdam Creek—2

This nice-sized stream runs about 25 to 30 feet wide just above the village of Sproul and is a state-stocked fishery. It looks like a freestone stream, but with 60-degree water in midseason. This stream shows signs of limestone influence. There has been some channelization, which could be repaired to give better holding water. While I didn't turn up any fish, the stream looks incredibly trouty. Paul Nale advises that the stretch from old Route 220 to Sproul is excellent "hog water," and I don't think he's speaking about the local agricultural practices. The limestone area is a relatively short distance above Sproul, but the influence continues on down to Claysburg where it joins South Poplar Run and becomes the Frankstown Branch of the Juniata. Construction of a sewage treatment plant eliminated the previous practice of discharging poorly treated effluent and gave the stream a major boost. Further stream restoration would help increase the trout population in the channelized sections of the stream.

Boiling Springs Run—3

This small stream is 10 to 15 feet wide and in places seems to be just as deep. Near Sproul, where I fished, the water was 58 degrees in late July but showed no other signs of limestone influence. Nevertheless, I am assured that farther upstream there are first-rate limestone spring creek areas, as well as a very well-preserved old gristmill.

A substantial section of the stream runs along a brickworks, and inevitably broken bricks cover the stream bottom. The water is discolored, probably due in part to the lingering effects of major road construction of Route 220, which might have been devastating had not the local TU chapter intervened to bring about some changes that much reduced the impact of construction and later runoff. There is good holding water, some deep holes, and wild browns, with a few wild brookies as well. I can't give a fair estimate, however, since the stream was off its form when I was there. This nice little stream contributes many wild fish downstream to Beaverdam Creek and the Frankstown Branch of the Juniata. Paul Nale says the best hatches are sulphurs, *Hydropsyche*, and *Tricorythodes*. But if you really want to clean up, a gold-colored spinner works all the time.

Brush Run—4

At around 20 feet wide, this is a substantial stream, but the paltry amount of decent holding water is full of chubs. The stream passes through Hollidaysburg, where it picks up lots of things people don't seem to want. Nothing attractive here, and no limestone influence.

Cabbage Creek—5

This tiny limestoner is really too small and too urban to interest any but the most fanatical fisherfolk. I didn't turn up any trout, but I didn't try very hard, either. The stream is generally about 5 to 10 feet wide and runs through front yards of urban row houses, which isn't my idea of a proper setting for a limestone stream. Nevertheless, the water is cold (61 degrees in late July), and there is a lot of aquatic vegetation and decent holding water, as well as clean gravel. There is even a waterfall in the lowest section, down near its confluence with Halter Creek, and wild browns, according to Paul Nale, who adds that there is a great sulphur hatch. Some habitat has been improved, presumably by the hard-working folks at the Blair County Chapter of TU.

Canoe Creek—6

This is a nice-sized stream—25 to 30 feet wide—just above the lake of the same name. It is pretty heavily stocked but also has a decent population of wild browns. A short distance above the lake the stream crosses the same limestone formation that gives nearby Mary Anns Creek its limestone character. In the case of Canoe Creek, the influence is much less apparent. The stream is generally shallow, but here and there, where the water flows over limestone ledges, there is good holding water and a nice population of trout. Stonefly shucks on the rocks speak well for the water quality. Blair County TU did habitat improvement here in 1969 and 1970, some of the earliest Trout Unlimited projects in Pennsylvania.

Clover Creek—7

The lower 5 or 6 miles of this fine stream are wild trout water with a good population of wild browns. This is a nice-sized stream, maybe 30 to 40 feet wide. When I was there at the end of May, the sulphurs were present and heavier than I had ever seen elsewhere. "Blizzard" is an overused word for such hatches, but it sure fits. There were loads of rising fish, great holding water, lovely pools, deep undercuts, and fine, fast water. The fish were anything but cooperative, and they thoroughly beat me. Quite a few of the rising fish were chubs, at least the ones I could convince to try my Ausable Wulff, but lots of others were clearly trout, and they were totally unimpressed with my efforts. But I can't knock the stream— it is beautiful, flowing through well-tended, rich farmland, and everything a limestone stream should be, except possibly cooperative, but it's not the fishes' fault if I wasn't up to them.

East Branch Piney Creek—8

This very small stream is a limestone spring creek, with frigid water (56 degrees in late July), loads of watercress along the edges, and other aquatic weed in the stream channel. It's only about 10 feet wide and maybe a half mile long at the most, and there has been some effort to "improve" it by channelizing parts. Cattle in the adjacent meadows do not help much, but, regardless, this is a nice little limestoner with wild browns. It could be a marvelous TU project, but it is far from shabby as it is.

Elk Run—9

This stream, a bookend to Huntingdon County's Logan Spring Run, which is across the valley from it on the same limestone belt, is very small—3 to 6 feet is the normal width—with some nice holding water. It is even smaller than Logan Spring Run, but these little streams hold a certain fascination—at least for me. Anyway, the trout are there, beautiful wild browns.

Fox Run—10

This is a sister stream to nearby Roaring Run. However, it is a bit smaller, less steep, and has fewer wild browns. Some homes along the stream detract from the fishing experience, but any stream that can support wild trout has something going for it.

Frankstown Branch Juniata River—11

This stocked stream is substantial, about 35 to 40 feet wide below

Sproul, and it runs cold, with 60-degree water in late July. Unfortunately, during the very wet summer of 1989 it also ran very high, although not too dirty. It has great holding water and a reputation for holding large fish. The only fish willing to take my nymph, however, managed to escape without being seen, and I suspect more weight would have helped get my offering down to the fish. This is a very nice piece of water, and, in spite of its relatively developed locale, I think the stream is worthy of more attention than I gave it.

Halter Creek—12

This small limestoner (20 to 25 feet wide) has been the object of a good deal of work by the Blair County Chapter of TU, and impressive deals have been worked out with Appleton Papers, which straddles it for some distance. The chapter has done an effective job because I turned up a few wild browns. A short distance upstream there is a fork in the creek, with the smaller tributary, Cabbage Creek, cascading down quite a substantial waterfall. There aren't many limestone waterfalls! The town of Roaring Spring features a lovely, large, spring-fed pond in the town park with sizable trout, strictly for ogling, cruising its weedbeds. The substantial flow of cold spring water gets pretty heavily used before it ends up in the stream. A potentially sensational trout fishery is heavily impacted, but the considerable efforts of the Blair County Chapter have paid off.

Little Juniata River—13

This reinvigorated river has suffered abuse for many years but has recently acquired a reputation as big-fish water, with heavy hatches of all the right mayflies. A kill a few years back did retard the rehabilitation, but this very large stream is fast gaining a well-deserved reputation as a fine fishery. Make no mistake, this is big water. Where I was, a bit above Spruce Creek, the stream is probably close to 100 feet wide, with deep, intimidating pools. This is no place to stumble around in after dark. The good news is that the fish are there.

The section from Tyrone to below Spruce Creek is in a limestone belt. In places the river swirls against high limestone cliffs, creating true leviathan habitat. Local legend is full of monstrous fish that have been electrofished up, or killed by poisoning, but they rarely have been caught. The limestone belt seems to have enough cold seeps to maintain good water temperatures (upper 60s to lower 70s) through the summer. While wading is the suggested way to get around, there are areas of deep, fast water and steep sides where either a hot-air balloon or a canoe are the only reasonable approaches. Wade carefully!

The insect life may conservatively be called prodigious. On a late May evening massive hatches of various sulphurs or March browns can kick off a brief but intense feeding frenzy. I have heard tales of green drakes, but as is often the case caddis are probably the real payoff. While I love to watch a mayfly drift along in stately grace drying its wings, and often disappearing below the surface in a subtle rise, the prolific caddis bring up very splashy and frequent rises, and they mercifully allow a certain degree of drag on the fly. Rumor has it that the white fly is also starting to show up in late August, which will add a new dimension to fishing this prolific stream.

I was not proud of the few fish I caught because they were such a small minority of the many I saw rising all around me. But Mark Nale indicates that this stream offers good fishing most of the year. He says between Tyrone and Spruce Creek the population is roughly 90 percent planted fingerlings of whatever year class and 10 percent wild fish, while below Spruce Creek it is roughly 50 percent wild fish and 50 percent stocked fingerlings. He also suggests the best year-round fishing is in this stretch. This river should be a definite stop on anyone's itinerary of the best limestone streams in the Commonwealth. Who knows, you might even land one of those monsters.

Mary Anns Creek—14

This small stream is only about 5 to 10 feet wide, although there are some pools that are a bit larger. It flows along the limestone trail in Canoe Creek State Park, which is a good sign. More exciting is the cold water. I caught only one wild brown, though I managed to help several others effect a long release. This is not a major stream, but it is a true limestoner in a pretty setting to keep in mind if heavy rains muddy the larger streams in the area.

New Creek—15

This little stream, about 6 to 12 feet wide near the confluence with

Canoe Creek, has cool water temperatures, good holding water in deep meanders, and a nice population of wild browns. I didn't turn up anything huge but got a certain satisfaction from handling good numbers of fish in a relatively short stretch of water. In the lowest sections, where the habitat is a bit shaky, the Blair County TU Chapter has put in some jack dams to create holding water. Though it lacks the aquatic weeds of a spring creek, this is a definite limestoner.

Oldtown Run—16

At 10 to 20 feet wide this is a nice-sized stream. Near its confluence with the Frankstown Branch of the Juniata it exhibits some limestone influence. It has cool water temperatures (64 degrees in late May), fine holding water, and wild browns. The stream apparently gets pounded—I noticed well-worn trails, bait containers, and some snagged and broken-off monofilament. But the fish are there in spite of the attention.

Piney Creek—17

This is a sort of junior varsity Clover Creek, which it parallels a few miles to the west. It is a bit smaller with not quite as many wild browns, although it does have a substantial number. It is also a likable stream, in attractive country, but not quite as pretty as Clover Creek.

My visit on an early August morning revealed a cloud of trikes bobbing and weaving over the stream. The water was still a healthy 60 degrees, and in short order five nice wild browns had attached themselves to my Ausable Wulff.

Plum Creek—18

This looks like a classic limestone stream, maybe 20 feet wide, flowing through rich meadows, with a number of large springs pumping fine, cold water into the stream. Everything is there but the trout. There are, however, a decent number of carp. This handsome stream has apparently been abused by a sewer plant high upstream as well as numerous cattle lower down, both problems that can be brought under control. Experience on the Letort shows it is possible to bring back a stream after similar abuse. This might be a well-known stream someday, since all the other ingredients seem to be in place. But for now, it can be bypassed.

Roaring Run—19

This tiny gem is pretty much vertical, and it does roar. There is heavy pocket water full of wild browns, and judging from the rafts of sulphur spinners in the eddies, this must be a prodigious hatch. The stream is quite small, only about 5 to 10 feet wide, but clearly has whatever is needed to support a fine population of wild browns.

Paul Nale says this stream continuously runs both cold and clear, two great attributes that explain those nice browns. He also says the wildflowers in spring are exceptional.

The lower, steeper stretch winds in and out of an old concrete flume, now broken up, which doesn't help the aesthetics, but it does put a historic stamp on the stream. It seems the flume is a remnant of Etna Forge, a major factor in national security, which merited a fort nearby for protection. That history has receded into the mists of time, but Roaring Run is a great little stream and worth a visit.

Robinson Run—20

This very small stream (5 to 10 feet wide) had cool water but such quantities of brush, mosquitoes, and chubs that I recommend you forget it. There is some limestone influence and there might be trout around somewhere, but with all the hassles and dense population of chubs—which time after time turn up in streams with few or no wild trout—I was easily discouraged.

Sinking Run—21

This nice little limestoner (maybe 10 feet wide) runs into the Little Juniata above Union Furnace. It has deep pools, good holding water, and good clean gravel. It lacks a lot in aesthetics in the lower sections, since it flows partly through a junkyard at one point and seems to be channelized up near Route 45. The only trout I caught in the lower section was a fine holdover, no doubt up from the Little Juniata. I was surprised and disappointed that I didn't see any wild fish. I should have gone upstream! Arch Spring waters this stream with about eight thousand gallons per minute through a natural bridge (thus "arch" in the name) in what is one of the most scenic areas in the state. Down to where the stream disappears underground (thus the name Sinking Run) there is some posted club water. I didn't visit this upper water, but I intend to go back and look for an unposted stretch.

Yellow Spring Run—22

This is a distant third in the trinity of tiny parallel spring runs that resuscitate Frankstown Branch of the Juniata River with jolts of cold water. It is very small, maybe 5 feet wide, has much less gradient and some siltation problems, and a few trout. In general it is a long step below Fox Run—very small, very brushy, and not much of a pleasure to be around.

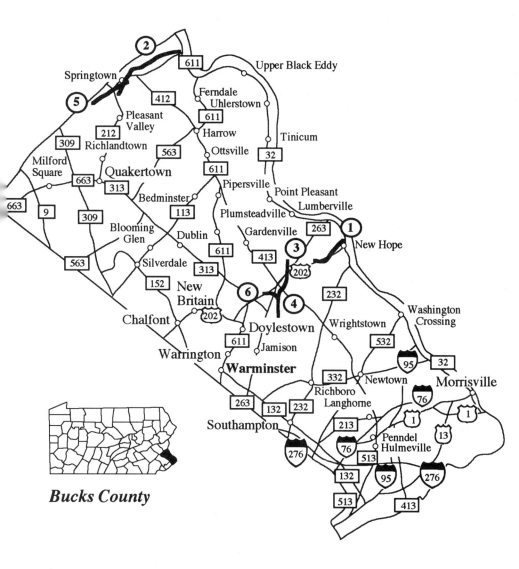

Springtown

Upper Black Eddy

611

5

412

Ferndale
Uhlerstown

611

Pleasant
Valley

212

Harrow

Tinicum

309   Richlandtown

563

Ottsville

32

Milford
Square

Quakertown

611

663   313

Pipersville

9

Point Pleasant
Lumberville

663

Bedminster

113

Plumsteadville

309

Blooming
Glen

Dublin

Gardenville

263

1

152

Silverdale

611

413

3

New Hope

563

313

202

New
Britain

232

Washington
Crossing

Chalfont

202

6

4

532

Doylestown

Wrightstown

Warrington

611

Jamison

Warminster

332

95

32

Morrisville

263

132   232

Richboro
Langhorne

Newtown

76

1

1

Southampton

213

1

13

276

76

Penndel
Hulmeville

513

132

95

276

513

413

Bucks County

BUCKS COUNTY

Growing up in nearby Chester County, I felt I knew all about Bucks County. It was a place half-populated by unattractive northern Philadelphia suburbs, the rest overrun by artists and New Yorkers looking for meaningful rural experiences. In short, it had little to recommend it. While that assessment is not totally wrong, it isn't totally right either. Much of the potentially marvelous limestone water in the county has been damaged by sewer plants or dams, but much of the county is rural and attractive. Cooks Creek in the far north is very rural, but upmarket in an area of well-kept farms and lovely views. The fish are lovely too. A stream like this is to be cherished and tenaciously protected, as the local TU chapter has been doing for some time. The other streams are TU projects-in-waiting. The potential is there, but so are the problems.

Aquetong Creek—1

This is a squandered limestone spring! Large springs feed an impoundment, which promptly warms up the cold water. Downstream the water was about 75 degrees on a cool evening in late July. The stream is about 20 to 30 feet wide and looks enticing. The 1775 Penn Map of Pennsylvania calls it Great Spring Creek, which it would undoubtedly be if someone would donate some dynamite for the purpose of removing the dambreast creating the impoundment. However, that doesn't appear imminent.

Cooks Creek—2

This delightful stream flows through rich farmland in the extreme northern part of otherwise urbanized Bucks County. It is a substantial stream, averaging maybe 40 feet in width. There are numerous small spring seeps that keep it cool all summer and provide what appears to be ideal trout habitat, at least for small and medium-sized fish. I didn't find anyplace where I might expect to hook up with the next state-record fish, but it is a lovely stream. Since this is wild trout water, it receives no stocking—at least officially. I turned up what certainly appeared to be a stocker brookie and a fat 14-inch rainbow with stubby pectoral fins. Nevertheless, the great majority were clearly wild browns and some smaller, wild brookies.

The appearance is largely of a freestone stream. Much of the streambed is made up of red sandstone washed in from the head-waters. There are a number of places where water flowing over major limestone ledges gives the appearance of a mountain stream, if it weren't for the surroundings of rich farmland and well-kept old stone farms and millers' houses.

There are good hatches, which bring up the fish. In season sulphurs are tough to beat, and a black ant does well all year, as it does on just about any limestone water. This stream doesn't get much notice, or pressure, because it's not really near anything. There is a considerable number of "No Trespassing" signs, but tactful permission requests are frequently honored.

None of the many fish I tangled with were large—about 12 or 13 inches being the biggest. Still, the chance to find good numbers of wild browns of that size, in that area, is nothing to sneeze at. The Cooks Creek Chapter of TU has a lovely piece of water.

Lahaska Creek—3

This decent-sized stream, about 15 to 20 feet wide, has cool water (66 degrees in late August) and lots of the right aquatic weed in the more open stretches. But there are no trout in evidence. A sewer plant seems to be the culprit. The locals say that the sewer plant frequently malfunctions—and it doesn't take much of a malfunction to eliminate the trout.

Mill Creek—4

This stream has a lot going for it, but it also has some problems. At about 20 feet wide, it is a decent-sized stream, and there are meadow stretches with all the right aquatic weed swaying gently in the subtle currents. With 65-degree water in late July, there are no thermal problems. Cattle have trampled parts of it flat, reducing the amount of holding water. But something else appears to be the cause of the lack of trout, a sewer plant most likely. The stream has potential, but whether the sewer plant controls the stream, and whether this can be turned around, isn't clear. It could make a great Trout Unlimited project if too much damage hasn't been done.

Silver Creek—5

This honest-to-goodness spring creek runs about 10 to 15 feet wide and gives a good jolt of cold, rich water to Cooks Creek.

There are several springs, including a very large one at Spring-town. The fishing is mainly in backyards in that town. There is good holding water as well as some generally unsuccessful "stream improvement." Why do we continue to think little dams will do other than what they always do, which is to widen and warm the stream and fill it with silt?

In spite of this—and the ultimate indignity of a "fishermen's contest," which mainly tramples the stream—there is a decent population of wild browns somehow struggling along. This is not a major stream, but wild trout deserve better than they get here.

Above Springtown there is what may be a unique opportunity: the possibility of fishing on limestone stream beaver ponds. Some Canada geese were feeling very territorial the day I was there, so I didn't push the matter.

Watson Creek—6

This small feeder to Mill Creek seems to be less in every way than the stream it feeds. It is maybe 6 to 10 feet wide and has been well and truly flattened by cattle, at least in the meadow stretches. In woods stretches it is simply impenetrable. The water runs slightly warmer than the main stream, but 67-degree water is still quite acceptable for late July. According to local rumor there is a remnant population of wild trout in the stream, but they didn't turn up during my visit.

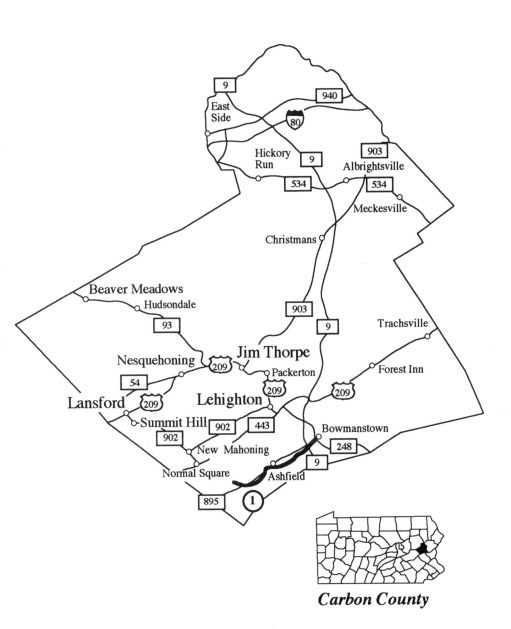

Carbon County

CARBON COUNTY

While there is some great fishing in Carbon County, none of it can be ascribed to limestone influences. This is basically a freestone area, with one narrow band of limestone running along Lizard Creek but giving it little influence.

Lizard Creek—1

This substantial stream is 30 to 50 feet wide and parallels a limestone bed. But it doesn't appear to have done the stream much good, since the water was hovering just below 80 degrees. It appears to be a classic freestone stream, with great pocket water. It's a shame the water is so warm. The stream is state stocked, but this is for the early season aficionado.

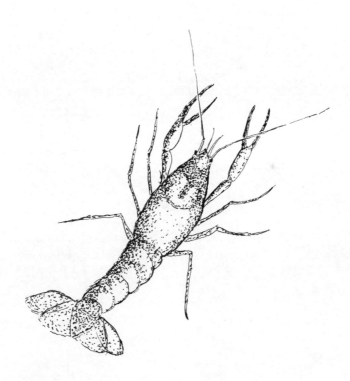

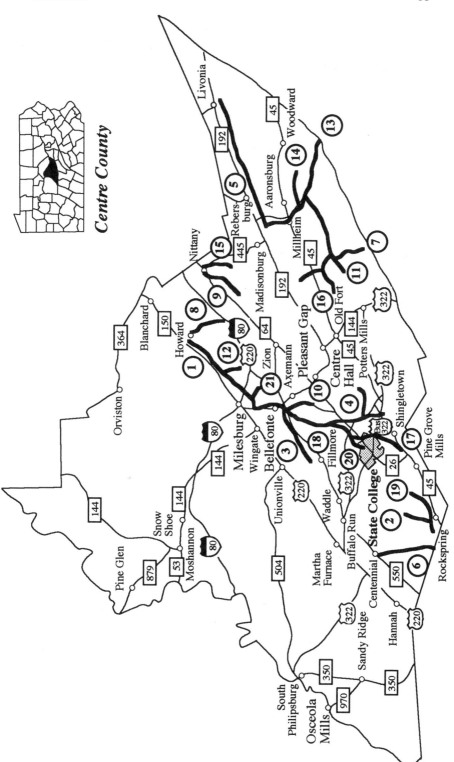

Centre County

CENTRE COUNTY

As was the case in many places, pre-Christian Finland worshiped a pantheon of gods. Fishermen prayed to Ahti for good catches. Given the climate in Finland, many of those fish would have been salmonids, so it is only a slight stretch to consider Ahti the god of trout fishing. If the religion still flourished and enough Finns had arranged for converts here, there would certainly be a shrine to Ahti in Centre County. This county has by far the best fishing in the state, and probably the East—and much of it happens in limestone streams.

The list is sort of an all-star parade of streams, any one of which would be drooled over if it were elsewhere. Spring Creek is probably the most popular with its connection to State College. However, Slab Cabin Run and Thompson Run also pass through State College. Nearby is Spruce Creek, water fished by numerous presidents and just about everything a limestone stream can be. Elk Creek, probably my favorite, is also nearby, as is the lesser twin, Pine Creek. These two streams combine their cool nutrient-rich flows and give a big boost to Penns Creek, perhaps the most famous limestoner in the Commonwealth. Lovely Lick Run and its smaller neighbor with the engaging name of Nittany Creek would be famous if they simply weren't overshadowed by their more prolific neighbors. Similarly, Logan Branch is one of the really great streams in the Commonwealth, although it is outshone by the many local streams of greater fame.

If you want superb trout fishing with prolific hatches and rafts of wild trout sipping down unfortunates, come to Centre County. These fish are not easy, but they are there, and some are huge. It's not by chance that a section of Spring Creek has been set aside as Fisherman's Paradise. But then just about the whole county is full of wonderful fishing, complete with exquisitely colored wild fish.

Cumberland County should not be put down. And Lehigh County, like Northampton County, has some astonishingly good fishing. Nevertheless, nowhere is there anything like the concentration of superb fisheries in Centre County. Some of these are spring runs with flat water, loaded with watercress for their length, and many others have sections fitting this description. This is the best place to try to commune with Ahti, the long-lost god of trout fishing.

Bald Eagle Creek—1

This stocked and very substantial stream (100 feet or more wide below Milesburg) could be considered "lower Spring Creek" since most of the water comes from Spring Creek with a few infusions of freestone water from Bald Eagle Creek. However, this stream is no Spring Creek. It is wide and generally shallow. It runs cool, due to Spring Creek's influence, but is not top trout water. Fishing the stream midmorning on Memorial Day revealed prodigious hatches of size 16 or so dun-colored caddis as well as a scattering of light-colored mayflies in the same size range. There were not many rising fish, and the only trout brought to hand appeared to be a freshly stocked brown. A rainbow managed to accomplish a long release, and others were either missed or made refusals that looked like takes. It may be stretching a point to include this stream at all since it doesn't flow over limestone. Nevertheless, the limestone influence, due to Spring Creek and to a lesser extent Nittany Run, cannot be denied. And while it is pleasant enough to fish, it's hard to justify spending time here rather than on the phenomenal streams nearby. In general, the hatches are better than the fishing.

Beaver Branch—2

This is the exception in Centre County, the one limestone stream that isn't worth much—because it is dry.

Buffalo Run—3

In spite of having a considerable amount of silt from a limeworks, this small feeder to Spring Creek boasts a very substantial population of wild brown trout. It averages 10 to 15 feet in width but has a good flow and cool water (65 degrees in early September). I didn't turn up any large fish, but I blame the stretch I fished, which had little suitable habitat. There were loads of small fish, up to about 10 inches, and they competed fiercely for my Ausable Wulff. No doubt this stream is a nursery for Spring Creek as well as being a nice little stream in its own right. The gradient is relatively high so there is a lot of fast water. This is one of the few places where I have seen a good hatch of honest-to-goodness size 14 Ausable Wulffs in mid-September. I have no idea what they were, but the match was very close.

Cedar Run—4

This is another in the long list of Cedar runs in the Commonwealth, just about all of which are excellent fisheries. This one is no exception. The stream varies from 10 to 25 feet wide and is classic limestone water with lots of wild browns and 57-degree water. A major feeder to Spring Creek, this is the way limestone streams are meant to be, though it's perhaps a little smaller than some might like. Anywhere else it would probably be a famous stream.

Unfortunately, about a year after I wrote the above description, some local fishermen indicated that the stream is for the most part posted (although I didn't see any signs when I was there), so be sure to check it out before fishing. It doesn't do any of us any good to enter posted land without permission.

Elk Creek—5

This stream is perfect. It runs cold all year long; it is nice sized, perhaps 25 to 50 feet wide; and it has interesting runs, nice pools, and occasional outcrops for the water to flow over. While the flow diminishes in midsummer, it retains plenty of water to keep fish in place, with temperatures in the low 60s. The insect life is good enough to bring fish to the surface, although I have frequently done better with nymphs. The wild browns, and a few wild brookies, are fine, fat fish. They are not easy to catch, but sometimes the fishing can be fantastic. I have not taken any really huge fish here—around 16 inches or so was my best—but I have seen some real bragging-sized fish edge out from brush piles to inhale emergers. It is a beautiful stream in a charming area, with a good head of wild fish. It's hard to write about this stream truthfully, as I'd like to say it isn't worth a hoot so no one will go there. With the Fish Commission's Project Future and the establishment of wild trout fishery management, stocking has been eliminated and, with it, much of the heaviest pressure. Streams just don't get much nicer than this one.

Halfmoon Creek—6

This small stream appears to have been heavily hammered in the past, probably channelized, and in parts demolished by cattle. It is 8 to 15 feet wide, but has little good holding water, lots of silt, and, in spite of its cold water (57 degrees), no fish of any nature visible. I thought it was sterile. Anywhere else this might be a stream worth getting interested in and seeing if it can be brought around. But in Centre County, with its bounty, this one will remain overlooked and abandoned to its problems. This is yet another stream where one of the Nale brothers, Mark in this case, took his spinning rod and, knowing what fools trout, caught decent numbers of wild browns.

Laurel Run—7

This small feeder to Penns Creek above Coburn is probably a freestone stream. When I visited I cast repeatedly to what I thought was a sizable trout nosing along under some overhanging grass. Eventually a muskrat swam out! I saw no evidence of trout or decent holding water.

Lick Run—8

Lovely Lick Run! From appearances, this small (8 to 15 feet wide) jewel is everything a freestone stream should be. It flows under the hemlocks, over ledges with plunge pools, and is gin clear. It also is a true limestone stream. It is a larger twin to Nittany Creek a few miles away. The stream is almost all in a nonlimestone area, but virtually all of the water comes from a limestone deposit, thus the limestone water quality in a freestone setting. The water is cold (57 degrees), and the wild browns are fat and numerous. It is stonefly water for the great majority of its length. In the uppermost sections it is a classic limestone stream, with deep pools, slow currents, and more wild browns. Streams just don't get any prettier than this. If it were a bit larger, it would be famous. Maybe it's just as well!

Little Fishing Creek—9

This medium-sized, stocked stream (about 15 feet wide) is a very distant fourth-string version of its larger namesake. While there is cool water (67 degrees), there are also cattle in it, which pretty well bombs it out. There are good numbers of wild brookies up in the freestone area, but the limestone area has really been mauled by the hoofed creatures.

Logan Branch—10

This feeder to Spring Creek is an important stream and in every way a first-rate upstate limestoner. The gradients are fairly steep, so none of the flats of the Letort or Big Spring are present. There are riffles, deep pools, and ravishing wild browns thriving in cold water (mid-60s). Apparently all sections of the stream do not share the same wild brown trout population. But where I was (which shall remain unpublished), there were loads of beautiful browns with bright red spots and adipose fins. They don't get a whole lot prettier. Apparently the stocked stream has a reputation for producing good numbers of very large fish, to the point where some night-fishing specialists have adopted it and, rumor has it, plundered it pretty badly. Still, it is a beautiful stream, even if the setting isn't always world-class (it runs right beside a road and past factories). It is worth a visit if you are in the area.

Muddy Creek—11

This small feeder to Penns Creek has none of the characteristics of a limestone stream.

Nittany Creek—12

A neat name for a little wild brown trout stream, but in reality this stream falls well short of the romance in the name. This small stream (5 feet or so wide) collects water from a good-sized watershed, where it flows underground until the geology changes and the water surfaces. The stream itself is not in a limestone belt, but its journey through carbonate rock is evident from the good temperature and the lovely wild browns. However, it is very small, brushy, and to some extent abused by cattle in the meadows it flows through.

Penns Creek—13

This very well-known stream runs in three counties—Centre, Mifflin, and Union—and the lower water is often called the largest limestoner in the state (although that claim is seriously challenged by the Little Juniata). But crowned champion or not, it is a large stream. The best-known parts are in the special-regulation catch-and-release area, which is mainly in the far northeast corner of Mifflin and Union counties. Here the stream generally runs 100 feet or so wide and has enormous pools that are often measured in hundreds of yards.

The stream is born at Penn's Cave, already a substantial stream when it comes out of the ground. It picks up size as various other feeders flow into it. At Coburn it receives the combined flows of Elk and Pine creeks, both fine streams in their own right, and it is pretty much full sized for its race through the narrows of the roadless area below.

While this is fine water, its accessibility allows pressure that might reduce the population somewhat compared to the really marvelous stretches downstream, below the limestone belt, but where the limestone influence lingers on. I regret that I might have missed some marvelous water in the upper sections, but the lower sections are so inviting that it is tough to drive past them to try elsewhere.

Much of the stream above Spring Mills is posted, but it appears productive. At and below the town there is true limestone spring creek water with wild browns, although the population does not appear to be anything like that in more remote stretches below.

The stocked stream is justly famous for incredibly prolific hatches, with the green drake the best known; but just about any hatch available in the East, from *Tricorythodes* to large stoneflies, is present here. The green drake hatch is really something special, and it draws a good number of fishermen. Classically occurring on Memorial Day (although a week later might really be a better bet), this flurry of insect life has to be seen to be believed. Marcia Drass, active in the Spring Creek Chapter of TU, reports that the green drake hatch coincides with sulphur hatches, and often the fish prefer the latter, at least for the hatching portion of the cycle. However, the fish key right in on the green drake spinners when they come down late in the evening.

In addition to the much discussed green drake hatch, the *Isonychia* hatch of late August and September is a great one to hit. The easy pickings excite the fish, and there are trout everywhere gobbling duns and spinners. This large and varied stream always seems to have something going on, with stonefly nymphs active in the heavy water or selective fish sipping terrestrials along the edges of some of the huge pools. If you look, you will find actively feeding fish somewhere.

Penns Creek has just about any kind of fishing that anyone could wish for. As the catch-and-release section is largely in a roadless area, there is normally plenty of room between fishermen, even in the green drake hatch. An old railroad right-of-way that parallels the stream offers generally easy walking in and out; however, surprisingly few people are willing to do this. In addition to the enormous pools there are lovely riffles and some heavy pocket water, which is a personal favorite, mainly because so few people fish it. The two really large fish I ever tangled with (and lost) on Penns Creek were both in pocket water.

Years of drought can be hard on the stream, as thermal problems will begin to develop, and the fish will enter feeders or hover around spring seeps, trying to stay cool. However, most years will give good fishing, with something hatching in profusion, right throughout the summer.

Parts of the stream are quite remote, giving a chance to feel what the area must have been like before mankind arrived on the scene. I've had a lot of miniadventures on this stream and have encountered wildlife I've rarely seen elsewhere.

One hot, real dog day in August, locusts were singing and occasionally falling from trees into the stream, hitting with a loud plop—generally followed by a frantic grab by the nearest trout. A friend was at midstream, so I stopped along the bank to chat. Soon it occurred to me that one of the locusts nearby was singing a bit flat. Out of curiosity, I turned—and noticed a coiled rattler about two feet away on the bank making a terrible commotion. Since wading wet is normal in midsummer, I was not dressed to tangle with such a critter. Needless to say, I moved—fast. Eventually I calmed down, but I'm ashamed to say that I did kill the snake. That won't happen again.

I don't want to give the impression that Penns Creek is loaded with snakes. In fact, that is the only poisonous snake I have ever seen in the wild, including many midsummer trips to Penns Creek. But it is an indication of how wild the special-regulation area is. One day on my way to a lunch break I rounded a bend and came face-to-face with a young bear splashing around in one of the stream's pools. I don't know which of us was more surprised. Another time a mink slipped into the patch of pocket water I was working and caught a fish (a chub fortunately) and proceeded to eat it like people eat ears of corn. I was in the catch-and-release area, but I didn't feel inclined to push the point. At other times ospreys have taken fish in my presence, deer have bounded away, and I saw the only porcupine I've ever seen in Pennsylvania. I have spent a good deal of time here, which may account for these encounters, but it is a remote area with little human intrusion—and a good head of fish.

The fishing is really good here, but with the unique surroundings it is only a part of the experience. Famous streams normally have a very good reason behind the legend. Penns Creek is
no exception.

Pine Creek—14

This model limestoner is a fine stream, but it is adjacent to the
more-famous Elk and Penns creeks so it doesn't get much notice.
The stream, like many other limestone streams, starts off a freestoner but runs underground when it gets into the limestone belt.

Marcia Drass indicates that the upper, freestone stretch of
this stream—before it disappears into the bowels of the earth,
leaving a perfectly good streambed with no water—has good fishing for small brookies and browns. It rises again, chilled and nu-
trient filled from classic "Jack Daniels" springs, in the lower valley and from there down is a classic limestone spring run (with
53-degree water in early September). Nice wild fish are present—
I can't comment on size other than to say I was unable to turn up
any really memorable ones—but nothing like the numbers in
nearby streams, in spite of what appears to be ideal habitat. What
the stream has going for it is less pressure than its neighbors, but
they are more famous for good reasons.

Roaring Run—15

This fine little stream (10 to 20 feet wide) is a tributary to Fishing Creek just about at the Clinton County line. It looks like a freestone stream, but has the water quality and temperature (60 degrees) of a limestoner. It also has wild browns and brookies. It is
not one of the truly memorable streams in this part of the Commonwealth, but that is only because of the extraordinary
streams in the area. It is a fine little stream, well worth including
on a trip.

Sinking Creek—16

This stream is about what the name implies: it sinks back into
bedrock, leaving a largely dewatered streambed with warm water
in midsummer. Though not an attractive piece of trout water, it is
stocked in some upstream sections, presumably to scatter opening-day pressures. Serious fishermen can bypass this one.

Slab Cabin Run—17

This is real limestone water substantial in size, about 30 feet wide, but dwindling down in the upper reaches to 5 feet wide—when the springs don't dry up. Steve Sywensky, who runs Flyfisher's Paradise in nearby Lemont, indicates that considerable stretches of the stream have been channelized for road construction, leaving little good holding water. That is true, but there are some stretches of pure limestone spring creek water with shoals of rising browns. This stream has some just plain lovely water, although it seems to run hot and cold as far as number of fish are concerned—there are either too many or none at all. But where they are, it's a marvelous fishing experience for wild browns.

Spring Creek—18

Is Spring Creek the best trout stream in Pennsylvania? Good question. Probably not, but you certainly could argue the point. By any measure this is an absolutely top-notch stream with miles of superb wild trout habitat. Its feeders—Cedar Run, Slab Cabin Run, Buffalo Run, and Logan Branch—are all excellent wild trout waters in their own right. A recent electrofishing exercise turned up a population of 250 adult trout per 100 yards of stream in one section—a standing population more than six times what's necessary to classify it as a Class A wild trout fishery. No question this is an impressive stream! The dark side is that this stream, like Chester County's Valley Creek (another outstanding wild trout fishery), has been contaminated, in this instance by the insecticides Kepone and Mirex, so the stream is under total "no-kill" regulation since the fish are health hazards. This regulation has been in place for a number of years now, and there is no evident overpopulation or stunting of the fish.

There are some posted areas and many where a streamside road somewhat diminishes the rural feeling of the place. Sewer plants also do their harm, especially below Houserville, and a major new sewer plant is to be constructed shortly below Bellefonte. However, the great majority of the stream is just plain marvelous fishing. It is a substantial stream, perhaps 50 or 60 feet wide in the middle stretches, smaller above and larger below. In the upper stretches there are definitive spring creek sections, while in the lower water there are sections large enough to make wading daunting, at least in rainy periods. There are good numbers of wild browns throughout, some probably huge given the excellent holding water, rich diet, and water temperatures in the mid-60s.

The area is getting built up, so this isn't really a rural fishery. On the other hand, it is a large stream, so even in periods of heavy activity there should be little problem finding a stretch that isn't crowded.

While Fisherman's Paradise is on this stream, there seem to be nearly as many, and as large, fish in less famous stretches. Pretty much any hatch you might expect to find on a limestone stream will be found here. Sadly, the green drakes are a thing of the past, but just about all of the others are here, although, as is normal, a particular stretch may be much better for a particular hatch than another.

In general trout fishing is just about finished at Bellefonte, and the lower stretches of the stream are pretty poor. While I turned up a few trout willing to impale themselves on my hooks, the conditions were less than ideal. My morning fishing on the good-looking fast water below the dam at Milesburg was discouraging. At one point I sat and watched a large sulphur dun floating down the flat water above the dam. I was curious to see if it would get airborne or get dragged over the dam and drown. It came closer and closer as the water quickened for the plunge. At the last possible instant there was a very majestic head and tail rise from a really large brown (best guess was about 20 inches), which settled the question. A futile effort to get into casting position confirmed there was no way for me to get to that fish, which is no doubt why it was there.

There is no question this is one of the very best limestoners.

Spruce Creek—19

This famous stream really comes into its own lower down, in Huntingdon County, but the upper portion is in Centre County and it is true limestone water. It's around 15 feet wide just above Pennsylvania Furnace and its impoundment. There was a lot of stream restoration work done there some years back, but at this point just about all the work is now in a state of disrepair. There are still some positive effects as far as holding water is concerned, though. There is good cold water (63 degrees), and when combined with good holding water, the fish are there, in this case an okay population of wild browns. Unfortunately, some backyard dams degrade the water by warming it, depositing silt in the riffles and spawning gravel, and impeding spawning migrations. I hope they will be removed, because while this upper reach is not as good as the stream lower down, it is still a good, solid limestone stream.

Thompson Run—20

Those familiar with State College know the duck pond, which in reality is sewer effluent—thoroughly gritty water that overflows from a silted-up impoundment. The ducks seem to love it, though. Some years ago the local TU chapter noted that the major spring feeding Thompson Run also discharged into this dismal pond, and with considerable effort they arranged to build a dike so the cold, clear water bypassed the pond. This, in essence, is Thompson Run. While the duck pond overflow still mixes with Thompson Run, there is more cold water than warm, dirty water, so it is something of a trout fishery. It gets better downstream and is quite good down in a growing water meadow. The stream is narrow and is tough fishing, but there are fish. I'm not red hot about eating wild trout, and with what must be coming into the stream from the duck pond, I think these fish are probably best left alone. However, they are handsome wild fish and a joy to fish over, especially if you like small streams (10 to 15 feet wide).

Unnamed Tributary to Spring Creek—21

This small stream looks very promising on the maps. As it turns out, this one is really small—tiny is probably an overstatement—and of no interest to fishermen.

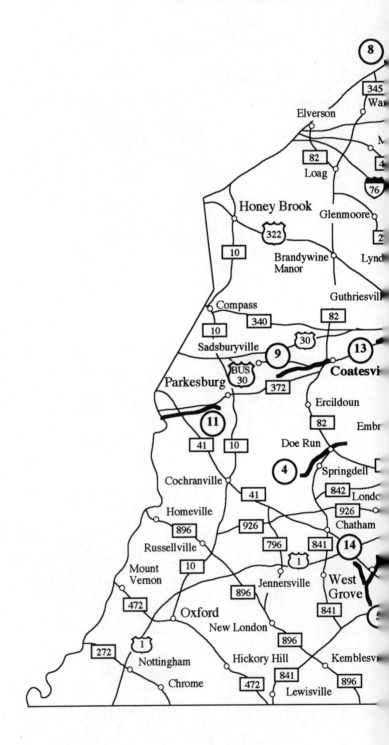

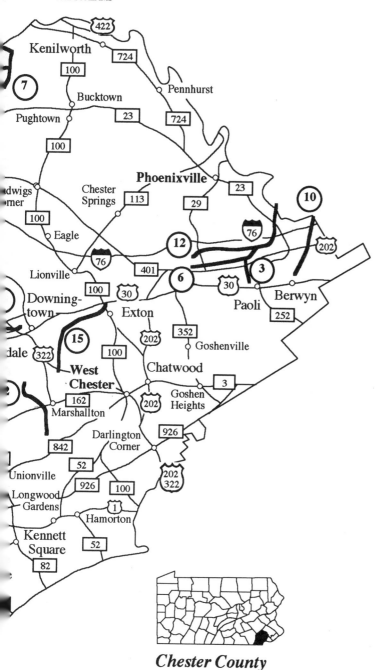

Chester County

CHESTER COUNTY

Chester County is losing its identity and being transformed into suburbs at an alarming rate, and the Quaker farmsteads that dot the hills now largely sprout new houses.

The main topographic feature is the Great Valley, which splits the county east and west roughly through the center. This long valley is generally a mile or two wide and has a limestone floor. While there are a few relatively unimportant limestone streams in the western portion of the valley, it is the eastern, and explosively developing, part that has the best water. Valley Creek, the stream that supplied waterpower to Valley Forge, is a superb wild brown trout fishery. But, though there are still some relatively remote sections of the stream—and its tributaries Little Valley and Crabby creeks—this stream is fast becoming an urban stream. Thanks to the limestone aquifer under the valley, however, flows and temperatures have continued in good shape. While PCB contamination has made this watershed a catch-and-release fishery, it is remarkable to find such high-quality fishing virtually on Philadelphia's doorstep. What is even more remarkable is the relatively little attention it receives.

West Valley Creek is a poorer sister to the west. It flows west rather than east, into the Brandywine, and runs for a substantially larger portion of its course out of the Great Valley, although the upper half of the stream is in the limestone belt and receives significant seeps from bone-chilling springs. It has suffered considerably from silt deposits for many years, so trout populations are small. Good quantities of nutrient-rich water influence the length of this stream. The lower sections flow through an idyllic valley largely protected from further development by generous donations of easements by conservation-minded owners.

While the fishing can be quite good in Chester County, it is hard to get away from the feeling that one is visiting a huge construction site. The jury is still out on the ultimate impact of all this development. If handled properly, it can be minimal, possibly even beneficial. Tenacious, ongoing efforts to protect these streams promise a bright future.

Beaver Creek—1

This is a nice stream, 15 to 20 feet wide, very reminiscent of West Valley Creek, which is across the Brandywine to the east. In mid-August it had relatively adequate water (71 degrees) and decent holding water. I didn't turn up any trout, despite persistent rumors that trout swim up into this nice stream to escape thermal problems in the Brandywine, which is stocked at that point. There was a very impressive chub population, and it is possible that the next state-record chub may come from this stream. If the chubs do that well, this should be fine trout habitat and a likely place for more stocking in order to spread opening-day pressures.

Broad Run—2

This pleasant meadow stream is around 10 to 15 feet wide, and while generally a freestone stream, it does flow over a section of the geological formation known as the "Cockeysville Marble," which gives it a jolt of cool water and brings it close enough to limestone to be of interest. The area is still largely pastoral but developing rapidly. If the Valley Forge TU Chapter prevails, perhaps a little less development will occur along at least one part of the stream. The water runs cool and has a good trike hatch. There are loads of chubs, but there are also some wild browns and a few wild brookies. The stream is characterized by meanders, with deep pools on the bends. Some parts are really overgrown and doubtless protect some large fish, which local legend indicates are in the stream.

Broad Run is all on private land, but a polite request can sometimes gain you access. This stream is not memorable except for its location in an area where there aren't that many wild fish. It's nice to know some still survive in spite of everything.

Crabby Creek—3

First, the bad news: as part of the Valley Creek watershed, this stream is under the "no-kill" rule imposed due to PCB contamination from the railroad yards at Paoli (the source of a lawsuit by the Valley Forge TU Chapter).

Now the good news: this tiny rivulet is a veritable trout factory. Recent electrofishing results turned up about one trout per running foot of stream. True, most of them were the young of the year, but they migrate down to Little Valley, and probably Valley Creek as well, and provide the great population of lovely wild browns there. At three to six feet wide, this stream is too small to fish enjoyably; however, it is cherished and has been the subject of a considerable amount of effort by our chapter. Construction of a new office park along the stream brought about lengthy, and ultimately very successful, negotiations to protect the stream. Ongoing discussions are being held to set aside critical lands upstream where the major springs rise to form the stream. A project is under way to create holding habitat and ease migration under some of the seemingly endless culverts crossing this short stream. We think we can substantially boost the numbers of young wild fish, which should pay dividends into the future. This isn't a stream for fishing, but it deserves all the protection it can get.

Doe Run—4

This is one of twin streams (the other being, naturally, Buck Run), and it also runs across the "Cockeysville Marble," which gives it some cold water. At 20 to 30 feet wide, it is a nice-sized stream to fish. Much of this stream flows through meadows, many of which were formerly in the King Ranch property. Although the stream warms up some in summer, it still harbors a remnant population of wild brook trout as well as the occasional wild brown. There are also some stretches that have some real behemoths stocked by local landowners who do not look kindly at people dropping in to fish. However, if you can gain permission, you can experience some good fishing. This is a beautiful stream in beautiful country, much of it permanently protected by conservation easements. Buck Run, although it is also a lovely stream, doesn't flow over the same marble substrate formations, so it is not as good as Doe Run.

East Branch White Clay Creek—5

Below Avondale this stocked stream is maybe 25 to 35 feet wide, but it appears to be blown out by poor storm-water management and a sewer plant. There isn't much holding water, and it has a sand bottom. It is another "Cockeysville Marble" stream. Above Avondale it is somewhat smaller and has better holding water. Although I didn't turn up any trout, I saw signs of some pretty hard fishing.

Little Valley Creek—6

This real gem of a small stream (10 to 15 feet wide) is a major feeder to Valley Creek, which flows through Valley Forge Park. It runs cold all year and has an impressive population of gorgeous wild browns, some sizable. The bad news, as with all the Valley Creek watershed, is the fish are contaminated and cannot be killed. This gives us a "no-kill" fishery with good numbers of wild browns right in the midst of an urbanizing area. It is not a flat limestone spring run, but rather is characterized by the pools, riffles, and meanders that are usually typical of a freestone stream. Nevertheless, it has many limestone springs feeding it along its length, keeping it cold. So far the stream has stayed siltfree, which allows good natural reproduction. The bottom mile is more or less open, while the upper sections are strictly private. The stream has undergone a number of devastating fish-kills, but it seems to bounce right back, a tribute perhaps to the quality of Valley Creek and its main feeder, Crabby Creek. If there is a deficiency, it is in insect life. There simply are no great hatches, only a mediocre sulphur hatch of short duration in May and sporadic hatches of other aquatic insects through the year. This puts a premium on fishing terrestrials, which is generally good throughout the year.

North Branch French Creek—7

This heavily stocked stream doubtless gets far more angler attention than any other in Chester County. There is a small limestone outcrop up along the Berks County line, above the stocked area. It doesn't really look like a limestone stream, although there is elodea in some places. I caught a terribly emaciated, stocked rainbow, which probably was a refugee from a put-and-take fishery either upstream or downstream, and didn't see any other signs of trout. Not worth another look.

Pine Creek—8

I fished here at the confluence with French Creek, where there is a small limestone lens. It doesn't do much for the stream overall, though. I didn't see any trout, although I did see a bunch of world-class chubs. I keep hearing rumors of wild browns in this stream, but I was unable to prove it.

Sucker Run—9

This poor little stream has been thoroughly demolished by the circumstances of its location. It is only 5 to 10 feet wide and maybe not worth mourning, but any loss hurts. Near its headwaters is a hazardous waste firm cited for chronic mishandling, downstream is a major steel mill, and in between are various truck parts, waste vegetables, and other refuse. This poor stream doesn't have a chance.

Trout Run—10

What a promising name—what a disappointing stream. It appears that naming a stream Trout Run is a form of death sentence, as the numerous streams of that name I visited during this project are now degraded, devastated remnants of what must at some point have been delightful little streams. Such is the case with this stream. It runs underground for parts of its course, and it runs cold, but it does not appear to have many trout. Once it ran cold and stable, but that was before urban development devoured the watershed of this small stream.

Valley Creek I (Atglen)—11

This is one of three Valley creeks in Chester County, and it is third in quality. It flows through the westernmost part of the same limestone formation that produced Valley Creek (Valley Forge), as well as Valley Creek (Downingtown). Quality definitely drops off as one travels west. This stream runs hot and is not trout water.

Valley Creek II (Valley Forge)—12

Will the real Valley Creek please stand up? Well this is it. It's about 30 feet wide and flows through Valley Forge Park. A surprising length of it between the park, Chesterbrook, Tredyffrin Township Park, and East Whiteland Township Park is accessible. The area is under intensive development, but this fine limestone stream survives. The good thing about this stream is millions of people live nearby and have the opportunity to fish over a good population of wild fish. Those floating "Xs" indicate where there should be fish holding—and they are there, although most have been caught a time or two and are not eager to repeat the experience.

On the negative side, there is a watershed-wide ban on taking fish due to PCB contamination from the railroad yards in nearby Paoli. Our TU chapter has filed suit, and a cleanup is in the works. In the meantime, this is a splendid catch-and-release fishery for some sizable wild browns (my best one last summer was 22 inches).

The stream has moderate gradient, typified by pools, riffles, and meanders. It is not a spring creek, but the numerous limestone seeps along its length keep it cool in summer. Urbanization is taking a toll, but the stream has been extremely capable of dealing with the various assaults.

Substantial insect hatches are sparse on this lovely stream, however. Midges hatch year-round and the dedicated midwinter fisherman can turn up a few persistent risers. The fly-fishing season begins in March with Blue-winged Olives, followed shortly by some Blue Quills, about size 18. The best hatch of the year is a tan caddis, sometimes locally referred to as the "opening-day" caddis, which pretty well pegs its timing. It runs through late April, when a lull occurs. The sulphurs produce great fishing for about a week in late May, whereas other streams in the area have a month-long sulphur hatch. There is a good hatch from about mid-September to mid-October of a small dun-colored mayfly, maybe a size 20 Blue Quill again. It can produce fast fishing over freely rising, unpressured fish.

The fish are generally in excellent condition, so we know they don't make a living sipping emergers. Like most limestone waters, there is a sizable freshwater shrimp population, as well as cress bugs in the quieter sections.

It is a lovely, historic stream. On peak spring weekends in the park there will be lots of picnickers playing Frisbee and listening to loud rock music, but you can get away from the noise and the people if you use a little ingenuity. The fishing is good. This is one of the major limestone streams in the state.

Valley Run—13

This small stream feeds Beaver Creek near Thorndale. It is about 10 feet wide, narrower in places. The stream has nice deep pools and cool water (68 degrees on a hot, humid day in mid-August). Persistent rumors have indicated that there are brook trout to be caught here. As far as I'm concerned these remain rumors. I saw some logjams that very possibly held trout but I couldn't prove it.

West Branch of East Branch White Clay Creek—14

As far as names go, this one's pretty complex. A nice meadow stream with decent holding water and temperatures, it is maybe 15 feet wide and, if not huge, certainly fishable. Unfortunately, no trout were in evidence the day I was there. There are probably some there, though, even if not in large numbers.

West Valley Creek—15

There is a lot of confusion when it comes to Valley Creek in Chester County—there are three of them, plus a Valley Run, all in the same limestone belt. West Valley Creek (popularly known as Valley Creek) flows west from Exton to the Brandywine. The upper four miles or so are in the limestone belt and give the stream much of its character: high-alkali content and relatively cool water in midsummer. Siltation is a major problem, which may in the future be minimized (the good news) by increasing urbanization (the bad news). The stream is 25 to 35 feet wide for most of its length, is heavily stocked, and gets a great deal of pressure.

As my home stream it will get more print than it probably deserves, but in order to protect it our TU chapter has put over five thousand hours into stream work and probably that much into meetings with government officials, so I will toot our horn a bit.

There is little natural reproduction due to the sediment load. Our TU chapter, however, has been working with Whitlock Vibert boxes for the past ten years and has gotten to know what we can—and cannot—expect from them. At this stage the chance of catching a stream-born fish late in the season is pretty good, maybe fifty-fifty in some stretches. The stream runs cool enough to hold fish well through the summer and has heavy trike hatches to keep them well fed. Heavy pressure does seriously deplete the numbers, but the fish are there all year for those motivated enough to go looking for them.

This stream has been badly abused, and many people are eyeing it for all sorts of uses now. It has hung in there, however, and continues to show astonishing recuperative powers.

As part of the exercise to get the DER's water-quality designation changed, which in turn led to this book, our TU chapter studied aquatic insects on the stream. We identified about twenty-five mayfly species, numerous caddisflies, and a few stoneflies. The insect life is excellent on this stream. The caddis hatch in midafternoon on opening day and produce reliable fishing. The sulphurs hatch prodigiously from the middle of May through the middle of June and produce fine fishing. The *Tricorythodes* hatch is heavy and much loved for its dependable fishing each morning from midsummer on. In addition to these mainstays, there are sporadic hatches of large, light-colored mayflies throughout the summer, visible on most evenings, as well as truly awe-inspiring

Hexagenia, which show up around dusk about the middle of August. While many others are also present, the sulphurs and the trikes are the major hatches for this stream.

In spite of all this fly-hatch talk, the Valley Forge Chapter of TU recently helped establish an "Artificials Only, Delayed Harvest" management stretch on the stream. This allows and encourages both fly and spin fishermen to enjoy fishing over a good population in preseason and early season, and then more or less dares fishermen to catch those same well-educated fish later in the year.

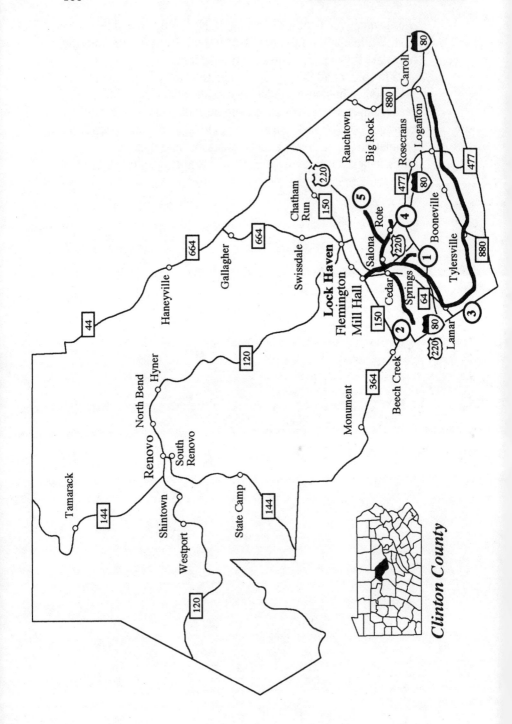

Clinton County

CLINTON COUNTY

By and large this is basic upstate Pennsylvania, with high, parallel ridges and generally tight valleys with well-kept farms. There are a few limestone bands, and they produce some exceptional fishing.

There isn't a lot of variety, at least if one wants to sample many different limestone streams. Fishing Creek and its two limestone feeders, Cedar Run and Long Run, are about the extent of what is offered. While Cedar Run and Long Run are good, honest limestone streams, they are simply overshadowed by Fishing Creek, which has some of the best trout fishing in the state.

Fishing Creek has it all. One of its lakelike pools produced Joe Humphreys's mammoth brown trout a few years ago. Its pocket water for stretches in the narrows is simply vicious with trout. Its many seeps and springs keep the whole length of the stream cold.

Central Pennsylvania is a laid-back place. Values tend to be pretty traditional, people are honest, and life is uncomplicated and free from problems facing the big cities. People are aware of the seasons, and opening days for trout and deer are important events. This is fine country with fine people, and as long as one doesn't mind being limited to only a few limestone streams, the fishing is superb.

Bell Spring—1

This small spring has been dammed up and loses any coolness it might have by the time it discharges into nearby Fishing Creek. This one can be skipped.

Cedar Run—2

This is a fine limestone stream, about 20 feet wide, with a good trike hatch, loads of aquatic vegetation, a 57-degree temperature, and considerable drops in some places resulting in fast, heavy water. I turned up one lovely 17-inch wild brown that liked my stonefly nymph in heavy water. I missed some others, and I was totally unable to interest the few rising fish that I saw. This is a fine unsung stream, which appears to be everything a limestone stream can be.

Fishing Creek—3

There are many people who believe that Clinton County's Fishing

Creek is the best trout fishing in the Commonwealth, and it's very hard to argue with them. Joe Humphreys's leviathan came from this stream, as have many other impossibly large browns and some improbably large brookies. About twenty-five miles of Class A wild trout waters offer far more fish than the required 40 kilograms per hectare. As might be expected for a stream this long, the lower sections are quite sizable, and some of the pools appear to be lakes, with little apparent current. While the stream with its many springs runs cool for its length, it does not appear to be a classic limestone spring creek. Rather, it resembles a freestone stream blessed with a lot of cold water. This is the first place I had ever seen a fog low over the water during hot, humid periods, although I have noted this occurrence quite often since.

There is a tremendous variety in this stream. Some of the upper portions—around and above Tylersville—are certainly reminiscent of limestone spring creeks. My first visit to Fishing Creek brought me to the bridge at Tylersville. I craned my neck over the edge and noted small brookies gobbling some minutiae. I also noted a lazy carp moving about below them. It took a while to realize that the carp had large black spots on its side and a red adipose fin. I didn't manage to do anything except terrorize that fish, but I got the idea.

Below Tylersville there is a stretch where the stream disappears beneath the surface for a while, leaving a nice-looking streambed with pools, riffles, and pocket water—just about everything that is needed except the water. There is another stretch downstream that also tends to dry out, but in between and below these anomalous sections is just plain marvelous fishing, in beautiful water, for gorgeous fish.

The narrows above Lamar is a section of great pocket water, with large numbers of trout embarrassingly tough to catch. Below that are mellower stretches of meadow water, where the cattle have not managed to abuse the stream too badly.

Below Mackeyville is an unnamed feeder that looked good on the maps but turned out to be totally dry. But Fishing Creek in that area is delectable with 62-degree water.

While there is a substantial special-regulation area in the upper stream, the whole watershed offers great fishing, with the open water perhaps being as good, since it gets less pressure. It is big water, and it is easy to leave other fishermen behind, especially if the idea of walking a ways from a road doesn't threaten. The fish are there. The great majority of those I encountered were browns, with just enough brookies to offer a pleasant surprise from time to time.

The stream appears to have just about every hatch anyone could want, including green drakes. Unfortunately, I missed the green drake hatch, but it is said to be outstanding. It must bring up some of the very large denizens of the deep holes and cut banks.

This may not be *the* best stream in Pennsylvania, but it certainly is among the very best, which ought to be enough for anyone. It's a pleasure to go to a stream that does better than its reputation!

Long Run—4

This fine little limestoner runs around 15 feet wide. There is a major spring just above the town of Salona that has a commercial hatchery sitting right on top of it. The effluent from hatcheries frequently is noted as inferior habitat, and this seems to be the case here as well. This stream looks and feels great, with 55-degree water in mid-July, but the only fish I could turn up were stockers. There were a lot of fishermen, most of them successful, all fairly unlikely for a morning in mid-July. Both Upper Long and Chub runs disappear into the ground and doubtless form the large spring that feeds the hatchery and Long Run at Salona.

Spruce Run/Chub Run—5

It is on the maps, but it is just a dry streambed.

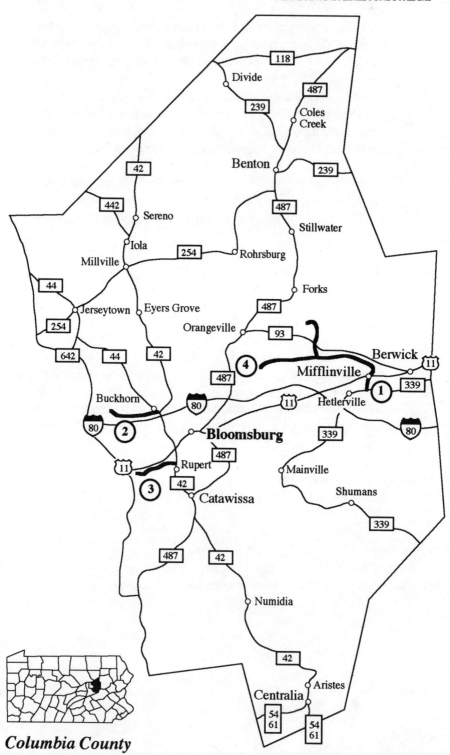

Columbia County

COLUMBIA COUNTY

In any list of areas with significant limestone streams, Columbia County must rank near the bottom. This is nice country, but it is typically north-central Pennsylvania ridge-and-valley country with virtually no limestone influence. There are some super freestone streams here, and they are well worth the trip, but go elsewhere for limestone streams.

Briar Creek—1

This is a nice, stocked stream, although I'm not convinced about any limestone influence. When I fished it, the water was up a bit and somewhat off-color. The water was cool enough at 68 degrees, but so was the air. There is good holding water, nice riffles and pools, and decent width (25 to 30 feet). There must be some trout there, but I couldn't raise one.

Frozen Run—2

With this great name, it conjures up images of seeps of frigid water and lovely wild brookies growing fat on abundant aquatic insect populations. But in reality the stream is pretty mundane. It is 5 to 10 feet wide and relatively cool at 68 degrees, but definitely not frigid, with loads of chubs. I wouldn't be at all surprised if it held some trout too, but I couldn't convince any to try my Ausable Wulff for breakfast.

Montour Run—3

This undistinguished small stream is 10 feet wide, with no obvious holding water. The water was warm and there were no fish except minnows. Not an impressive stream.

West Branch Briar Creek—4

The day I was there the water was nice and cool at 68 degrees, and there were good numbers of trikes in the air above this modest stream. The stocked creek is around 15 feet wide, and it looked as if it should hold some trout. But if there were any, they didn't like trikes. The naturals were gobbled by minnows but were unable to pull any substantial fish of any kind to the surface. It does not appear to be a limestone stream.

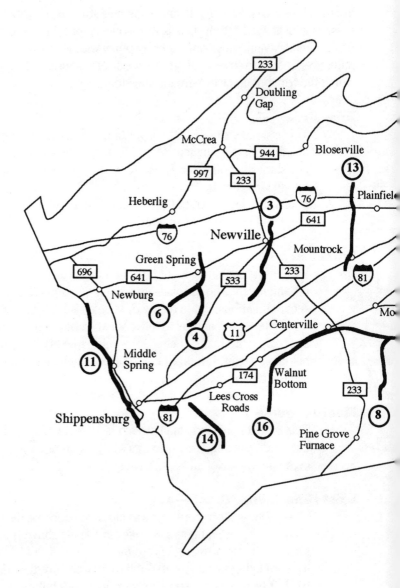

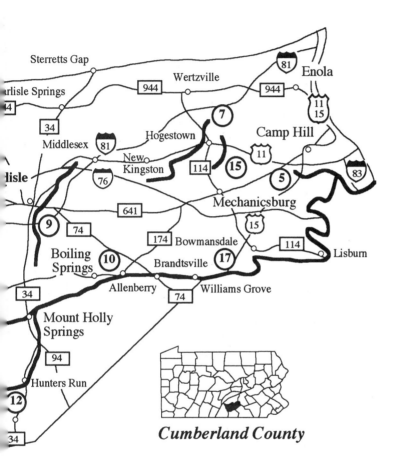

Cumberland County

CUMBERLAND COUNTY

This is the classic area for limestone stream fishing on this side of the Atlantic. Its spring creeks are legends, instantaneously recognized by serious trout fishermen around the country and overseas. The Letort ranks at the top of the list. Due to the abuses caused by development along its shores and the haphazard use of pesticides, in some ways this stream may not be as good as it was. By any standard, though, it remains a famous fishery, with good numbers of incredibly selective wild browns. The good news is that sewer effluent no longer drains downstream, so we have regained a few miles of great trout habitat.

The county features a wide central area with a relatively flat limestone belt. The Letort is here, as is the Yellow Breeches, a heavily fished stream in a lovely setting. It may not be up to its fame, but it is an important stream in many respects. Green Spring and Big Spring are definitive limestone spring creeks. Each has suffered some abuses, but both are marvelous fisheries. Diminished only by their proximity to the Letort, these spring creeks are in their own right superior fisheries.

There are other fisheries, less famous but just as fine, perhaps even finer. I love Silver Spring, although it is very short and cannot handle much pressure. Cedar Run is still a very respectable stream, even though it's a shadow of its former self. Middle Spring Creek, which straddles the county line in the town of Shippensburg, is a great fishery—if you don't mind dodging the police, since no fishing is permitted in town.

Cumberland County is a rich land full of old farmsteads, a few still growing crops of wheat and corn. Virtually on Harrisburg's doorstep, the better-known waters tend to be crowded—sometimes very crowded—on popular weekends. The trip is still worthwhile, especially if you want to experience limestone stream fishing in the classic sense. Although I prefer the less-pressured upstate limestone waters, a visit to Cumberland County is a must.

Some American fly-fishing legends have known and written about these waters. Vince Marinaro and Charlie Fox, two wildly different personalities who have complemented each other in their studies and efforts to protect their beloved streams, top the list of local fishing personalities. Others have now begun to pick up their work, and they have a great place to expend their efforts.

Alexander Spring Run—1

This is a ditch in a meadow. The water was 77 degrees when the air was 78. Not trout water.

Barnitz Run—2

This very brushy little stream, for the real small-stream aficiona-do, varies in width between only 8 and 12 feet. There are numer-ous signs of limestone influence, but it is not a spring creek and it doesn't have a lot of good holding water. A few wild brookies survive where there is a niche for them.

Big Spring Creek—3

This is one of the epic limestone spring creeks in Pennsylvania. It is fed by an enormous spring and a few other springs downstream to keep the temperature tolerable. It is steeped in history and is a must for anyone who wants his limestone stream passport stamped with all the classics.

    This stream will probably give you the best chance to catch a truly large wild brook trout in Pennsylvania. In spite of a lot of competition and some water quality problems, there is a popu-lation hanging on in the uppermost water. These fish get quite large and are anything but easy to catch. At the spring head there is a major fish hatchery, now run by the Fish Commission, which appears to be something of an embarrassment, as the waters coming out of it are less than pure. There appears, also, to be a problem caused by hatchery trout, which have escaped and pop-ulated the uppermost sections of the stream, severely crowding the resident brook trout population. The Fish Commission rec-ognizes both these problems and is trying to get the situation un-der control, but at the present time the hatchery is doing dam-age to this important water.

    There are a few other problems as well. A short distance down from the hatchery is a long stretch about four streams wide but only one-quarter stream deep that acts as a solar collector, al-lowing the stream's precious cold water to be warmed up. Plans are under way to constrict this area in order to improve the habi-tat and dramatically increase the holding population in this and downstream sections. The uppermost water has already been constricted, and it is narrow and deep and holds enormous num-bers of trout of the common varieties. These fish are difficult to

catch, having been subjected to just about every type of fly fishing possible, but from time to time one will make a mistake.

Downstream there are more first-rate spring creek sections,
with somewhat looser regulations than those on the uppermost
waters, where only fly fishing is permitted. As the stream flows
downstream, the lower sections suffer some thermal problems
and are mainly stocked, but from time to time a few meticulous
anglers take some real behemoths because they understand how
to drift a scud imitation just right.

This is an important stream—not without its problems. But
changes are under way to return Big Spring Creek to its former
greatness.

Bulls Head Branch—4

This likable limestoner is a major tributary to Green Spring, one
of the more frequently mentioned limestone streams in Cumberland County. A pretty stream, although quite short, maybe a half
mile total, it varies between 8 and 20 feet and in places is an absolutely classic limestone spring creek with 52-degree water. I did
not see many fish, but with the cornucopia of foods available,
they really don't have to surface feed. The only fish I turned up
was a stocker brookie.

Cedar Run—5

Charlie Fox has praised this stream as the finest small limestoner in the Commonwealth. No doubt it once was, but land-use
changes have made an impact. The upper water is an exemplary
limestone spring creek, but it runs in a channelized ditch behind
truck-repair places. The middle stretch is a prison, with some
large ponds that are great for ducks but not for trout. Below that
is a moderately built-up area where the stream flows through suburban backyards. It's all very discouraging. The only part free
from damage is the short bottom section just above its confluence with the Yellow Breeches. This is an extremely steep stretch
of water with a few waterfalls. Not a large stream, 20 feet or so
wide, it has excellent holding water for fine wild browns, as well
as a few stockers that must have come up from the Yellow Breeches to enjoy the 65-degree water. It isn't easy fishing, but the fish
are there, and I think some are quite large. Nevertheless, even this
lowest section is far from a wilderness experience, with homes

and other buildings heavily crowding the stream. Perhaps in a different location this might be a famous stream.

Green Spring Creek—6

This is another limestone spring creek of Cumberland County. It is, however, slightly off the beaten path, and as such it gets less pressure than its slightly more famous kin. One place to avoid is the side that goes up along the west bank opposite the substantial cress farm near the confluence with Bulls Head Branch. This side is a green hell of multiflora rose.

The fishing is pretty much what you'd expect. The stream appears to have a small wild fish population, but the stockers seem to thrive and they become selective pretty quickly. There is a decent sulphur hatch in mid-June and presumably before that as well. Not a large stream, maybe 20 feet wide, it does not give up its fish easily, at least at midday, but in the evening you might find a sipper or two willing to make a mistake if the presentation is right. It's a good, honest stream, but with the lack of wild fish and 68-degree water, it is overrated compared to the really marvelous limestoners out there.

Hogestown Spring Run—7

This stream was a major disappointment. It is a model little limestoner, 15 to 20 feet wide, with lots of the right kind of aquatic vegetation, overhanging grasses, and frigid water (57 degrees) from large and frequent springs, but near as I can tell, no trout. What's the problem? It's worth some investigation to find out since everything seems to be in place except the fish. Solving this mystery could take pressure off the other limestoners nearby.

Kings Gap Run, South Fairview Run, Coblersville Run—8

These three streams are alike. All show limestone influence, but all are tiny, have banks covered with heavy brush, and are probably unfishable, even by small-stream fanatics. Like nearby Barnitz Run, they might have a population of wild brookies, but they are protected and will no doubt remain so.

Letort Spring Run—9

The Letort is arguably the most famous limestoner on this side of the Atlantic. It is a substantial stream, up to about 40 or so feet wide and several miles long. Most of it is accessible, except the part that flows past the Army War College. This is the hallowed water of Charlie Fox and Vince Marinaro, the laboratory for much of what we know about special tactics for spring creeks. To be here, especially on the upper water, is to be in a special place in angling history.

While the past is glorious, the present is also very fine. A fish-kill a few years ago did terrible damage, but the trout are coming back strong, and in a few years this event will be a memory. The fish here are wild browns, although there is some stocking in a stretch near Carlisle. A special strain reaches prodigious size, and maintenance of this strain was the reason restocking was so fiercely resisted after the kill. Opportunists that they are, the remaining wild browns quickly filled the void.

The upper water is a classic spring creek, and the currents are slow but powerful. The bottom is generally muck, caused by aquatic vegetation trapping and piling up silt over the years. All that aquatic vegetation provides a home for innumerable freshwater shrimp and cress bugs, which form the major part of the wild brown's diet. Hatches of aquatic insects are generally sparse. While the fish instinctively keep their heads down and pig out on the underwater fare, remember too that this is pretty much where terrestrial fishing began, so fishing dries is not a waste of time.

As the stream enters Carlisle, it gets compressed between rock walls and loses most of its appeal. However the recent removal of a sewer plant has opened up a number of miles of very good, if somewhat inaccessible, fishing below Carlisle. The previously mentioned stocked water is in this section, but more remote stretches have wild fish, with all their fins and glorious colors. These lower stretches, especially the improbable stretch of pocket water at the very bottom of the stream, do not appear to get much pressure. You'll find numbers of carp, accompanied by a fine population of wild browns. Admittedly, fishing pocket water is not why many people come to the Letort, but try the lower stretch—the fish there don't get near the pressure as up above.

I don't want to dissuade anglers from going to the upper waters; simply walking along the stream is a spine-tingling experience.

Little Run—10

This nice-sized stream (20 to 30 feet wide) is well named. It only flows for about 200 yards, from the dam at the Boiling Springs lake to the Yellow Breeches, where it still has enough coolness to influence much of the special-regulation water. Little Run is under special regulations and is just teeming with fish, mostly stockers who know all about leaders and are tough to fool. Don't come here expecting a wilderness experience; fishers here measure elbow room in yards rather than miles. Nevertheless, Boiling Springs is a lovely area and the fishing is great.

Middle Spring Creek—11

Straddling the line between Cumberland and Franklin counties, both great areas for limestone streams, is a potentially great limestoner. It has a few problems, however. No fishing is permitted within Shippensburg, and just below the town is its sewer plant, which, like so many others around the Commonwealth, degrades the stream below its discharge point.

The stream continues for quite a few miles below Shippensburg. Below the village of Middle Spring, where I fished, it is an appreciable stream 40 feet or so wide and is stocked. However, by midsummer, when I was there, the fish had left and the temperatures were nudging toward the danger zone.

The first time I visited Shippensburg, I stopped on the main street and looked over the bridge traversing this stream. I thought I had died and gone to heaven, as there were fair numbers of rising trout, some real dandies. I went downstream a short distance, where it was a lot easier to get into the stream, and discovered a lovely limestone spring creek complete with gorgeous wild browns, as well as a few brookies and rainbows, which probably were hatchery products. The water was cold, the gravel was clean, and even if the water ran next to someone's house, this stretch was a major find. In relatively short order I caught about a dozen fish, up to 18 inches long, and I felt that I had located an overlooked spring creek, which in a way I had. I returned a few weeks later, and in fairly short order was accosted by a police officer who suggested that I shouldn't fish there—only it was a bit more forceful than that—and implied I was messing around with the town pets. Apparently everyone else knew all about those fish. There was even a small dime-operated machine beside the bridge where townsfolk could buy trout food to throw to the fish. No wonder they liked dry flies!

The long and short of it is, the town fathers will try to replace the "No Fishing" signs that were missing when I was there, and those fish will remain naive about hooks all their lives. It's a shame such a neat stream is posted where the fish are not damaged by the sewer plant.

Mountain Creek—12

This stocked stream more or less follows a limestone belt most of the way from its headwaters down to its confluence with the Yellow Breeches, a distance of probably ten miles or so. Much of the middle water is wide, shallow, and populated by carp. In spite of many cold-water seeps, which kept the stream water temperature at about 72 degrees on a very warm, humid day, there was no evidence of any trout or any likely looking places for them. Below Mount Holly Springs it was cooler, around 70 degrees, and looked more like trout water. I turned up one good 13-inch wild fish that had the brown trout's typical fascination for Ausable Wulffs floated in fast water. However, that was the only trout I moved in some distance. The stream looks good, but it sure has a sparse trout population.

Mt. Rock Spring Run Creek—13

This stream is tiny and not trout water.

Thomas Run—14

This is basically a dry streambed—its flow diverts to contribute to Middle Spring.

Trindle Spring Run, Silver Spring—15

Trindle Spring Run itself doesn't amount to much and isn't worth searching out. But Silver Spring is everything a spring creek should be, except that it is short. It flows only about a half mile from its major springs to the confluence with the Conodoguinet, where on a humid day there will be a low-lying fog over that side of the river for several hundred yards downstream.

The spring flows beneath Route 11, which at that point is a commercial strip between used car lots and contractors' offices. It is disconcerting to fish while eighteen-wheelers change gears right above. The lower part of the stream, fortunately, is in a park and offers some pastoral experience, which is much enhanced by the quality of the water.

Silver Spring is simply gorgeous water, about 30 feet wide

and crystal clear. It runs frigid, with 55-degree water all summer. It has clean gravel and loads of watercress, elodea, duckweed, and other aquatic vegetation slowly swishing back and forth in the current, which at times is quite fast due to a relatively steep gradient, and at other times gentle and seductive.

Such beautiful water simply has to have trout in it, and it does. While plain ineptitude on my part, together with the weeds, made me lose many of the fish I tangled with, I did catch a number of wild rainbows. I also caught a fine fat brown, which appeared to be a swim-up stocker that had put down roots. It had lovely red spots but mangled pectoral fins, so I figured it was a Fish Commission product.

The rainbows that I landed appeared to be of the same year class and, at 8 to 10 inches in August, were most likely less than a year old. I lost one really nice rainbow, but I didn't get it close enough to comment on its origins. There is a lot to eat in this stream, so fish grow rapidly.

I tried hoppers in hopper season and got only half-hearted refusals. Going down after them proved far more effective, as might be expected in this natural supermarket.

Referring to old newspaper clippings, I discovered that Charlie Fox had written about Silver Spring and about how good it was in the old days (the 1830s). It's still a gem, and it demands protection as a unique resource. It is short enough that it cannot stand much pressure or many fish being taken out without seriously depleting it. But how to give it the protection it deserves without bringing down rapacious hordes? While I fished in total isolation (I didn't even see any bootprints), there were mobs on the Yellow Breeches waiting for the white fly to appear. I don't like fishing with hordes of people, and I hope notoriety won't wreck this lovely stream. My larger concern is that someone might unknowingly wreck this water while no one is watching.

To have such a jewel within five to six miles of Harrisburg is just incredible. That it remains apparently unknown and unloved is even more so. If you want to sample limestone spring fishing the way it used to be before they were discovered, hurry to this one. It deserves high praise and protection.

Walnut Bottom Run—16

This is yet another clone of Kings Gap and other runs that feed the Yellow Breeches. It is also cold and tiny. Perhaps it holds some wild brookies, but they will be safe from me. Even with my 6-foot rod this stream is too small.

Yellow Breeches Creek—17

What a great name for such a disappointing creek. This is a long and much-storied stream. In the lower sections it reaches substantial proportions, 60 to 80 feet wide, but apparently is better suited to carp than trout. This is basically a stocked stream with very limited natural reproduction. While some enormous fish have come out of this stream, in general they didn't reside there very long.

The white fly of August is the most famous hatch on this stream, generally due to the lack of other major hatches at that time of year. The stream gets a great deal of angler attention, especially at Allenberry Playhouse in Boiling Springs. This might be the ultimate in clubby fishing, a chance to show off the newest gadgets, but basically it is fishing in relatively crowded surroundings for stocked fish. On the other hand, other streams in the area are spared this intense effort, perhaps to their relief. While you may want to check out this famous stream, leave plenty of time to get to a better stream in the area.

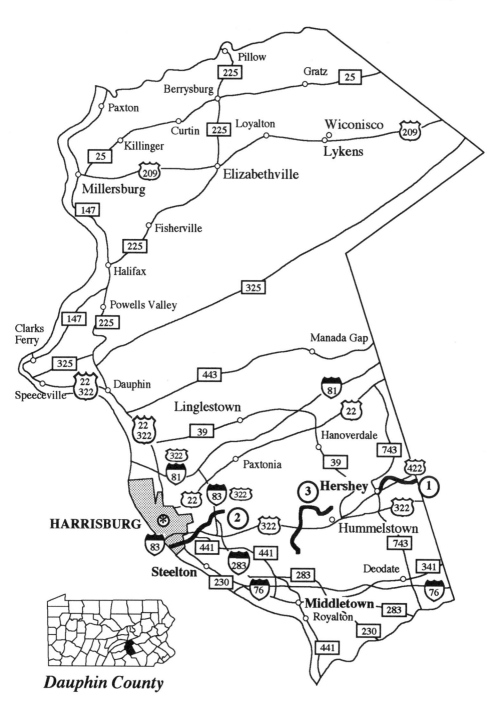

Dauphin County

DAUPHIN COUNTY

A considerable amount of the southern parts of this urbanized county is underlain by limestone, and, since this is where most people live, there has been a number of land-use conflicts. The streams have suffered.

Two of the county's limestone waters are named Spring Creek. Although heavily urbanized and running through backyards and golf courses, one seems to be basically intact and holds at least a few trout. The other appears to be bombed out, but it could become a TU "superproject."

In general, as far as limestone stream fishing is concerned, Dauphin County is a place to come from, not to go to.

Spring Creek I (Hershey)—1
This very pretty stream flows through Hershey—the town and the factory grounds. It's around 25 to 35 feet wide and is true to its name. A fair length of it runs through golf courses, which diminish the overhanging brush a little, but it has decent holding water and good water temperatures. As is often the case with streams near golf courses, there are a lot of golf balls in the creek. What there aren't, however, are a lot of trout. I fished a good long stretch of the stream, since it looked appealing. I saw chubs and carp in the lowest section, and up above the factory I eventually turned up a stocker rainbow. The stream is nice, the habitat looks good, but frankly it appears to be wasted as a trout fishery.

Spring Creek II (Harrisburg)—2
This midsized stream (about 25 feet wide) right in Harrisburg has good cold temperatures and decent-looking holding water. It also has festoons of trash, and a few of the better holding spots are beside shopping carts. This is a bombed-out limestone stream. The water is clear and cold, but there could be just too much urbanization to overcome. Sewage in the area may be a problem as well. I saw some minnows and a few chubs, but not much insect life. This could be a dream TU project if some chapter is looking for a very tough situation. Until this stream gets a lot of love, it is a write-off.

Swatara Creek—3
By the time this major stream gets to a limestone area, it's about

100 feet or more wide and is territory for smallmouths and probably muskellunge, but not trout. It is slow moving, normally muddy, and relatively warm.

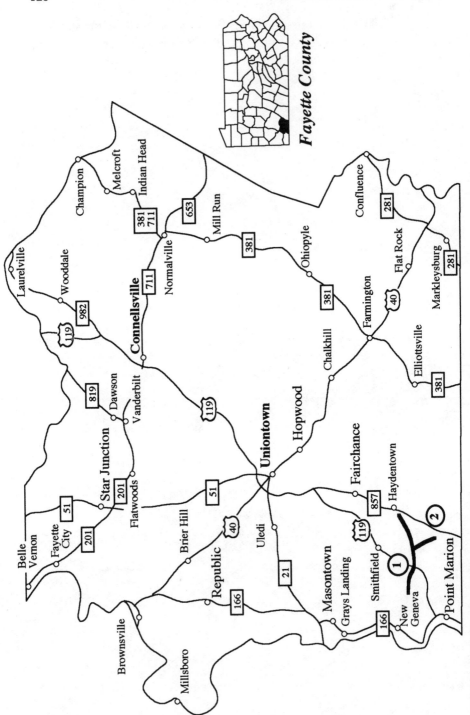

Fayette County

FAYETTE COUNTY

This area is well beyond what is normally thought of as the limestone territory of Pennsylvania. Nevertheless, the longest cave in Pennsylvania is located here, and other evidence of limestone demanded a visit.

Georges Creek—1

The 1775 Penn Map calls this stocked stream Limestone Creek. There are signs of limestone (some cobbles are limestone, and there is limestone near the headwaters), but the main stream has lost virtually all the limestone influence. Unfortunately, an acid mine drains into the stream. This substantial stream is really smallmouth water. In midsummer it runs too hot for trout, even in the wet summer of 1989. At 40 to 50 feet wide it is an impressive body of water, but the thermal problems are just too much to handle.

Mountain Creek—2

This stocked creek appears to be a freestone stream; however, Laurel Caverns, the longest cave system in Pennsylvania, is near its headwaters. A number of the cobbles in the streambed are limestone, and while it doesn't run cold in summer, it is cool enough (mid-70s) to hold some browns, some perhaps are wild. No small ones turned up, but some of the keeper fish looked for all the world like naturals. This is a pretty stream, maybe 20 or 30 feet wide, with nice riffles and pools and overhanging vegetation to give refuge to spooky fish. *Isonychia* shucks were much in evidence in late July. While it is no spring creek, it is a nice stream with some limestone influence.

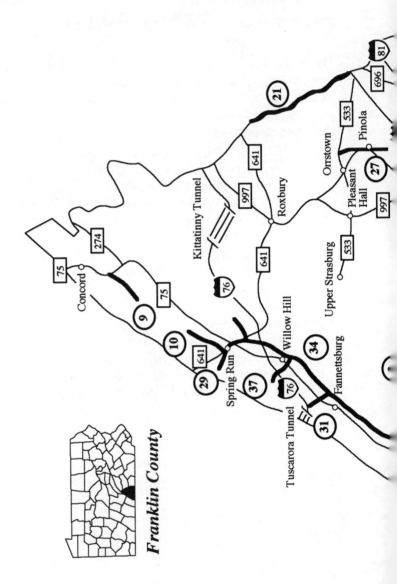

Franklin County

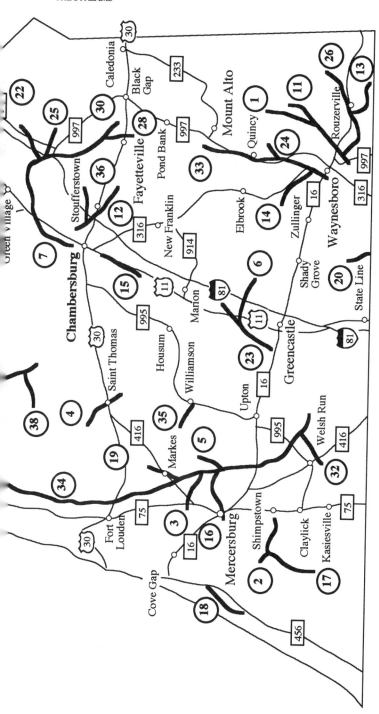

FRANKLIN COUNTY

Before I had ever knowingly set foot in Franklin County, I knew of Falling Spring Branch as one of the important limestone spring creeks of the Cumberland Valley. It deserves its fame, but it also could use some restoration, especially at the lower end.

There is, however, much more to Franklin County than this famous stream. In sheer numbers of limestone streams, Franklin County comes in second to Lancaster County. What is more impressive, though, is the number of potentially great streams located here. While cattle have diminished the quality of some of the streams, lack of attention has probably hurt more.

Rowe Run, Church Hill Spring Run, Spring Run, Dickeys Run, and Marsh Run are all classic limestone spring creeks in need of friends. With a bit of work all of them could be healthy and famous. It is encouraging to know that we are not out of limestone streams, but there are several out there in need of help. And we are limited only in the number of people willing to get involved!

Franklin County also has its share of potentially great water sacrificed to sewer plants. Middle Spring immediately comes to mind. We need to find ways of dealing responsibly with our wastes and not killing streams in the process.

This large and varied county appears to be virgin territory for the adventurous seeker of limestone waters. You will find no footprints along a number of these streams, and the fish will not have cauliflower ears as do those in hard-pressed waters. This is a very pleasant place to spend some time and a rewarding place to put in some effort fencing cattle away from streams or removing sewer plants.

Biesecker Run—1

While this stream has some limestone influence, it is too small to be fished.

Big Spring Creek—2

This stream belies its name, being only 6 to 8 feet wide, but it has nice holding water, good cold water, and enough aquatic vegetation to make the proposition of limestone plausible. It also has the largest sycamore tree in the world at its mouth. It doesn't have trout.

Buck Run/Dickeys Run—3

This is an important limestone stream. It originates from very small feeders on the mountainsides to the west and is a very small stream until it hits a number of major springs a short distance above the Mercersburg Sportsmen's Club. Below the club it is a good limestone stream, with lots of aquatic vegetation in the slow stretches, fine pools and riffles, impressive limestone outcroppings, and 60-degree water. There has been some major stream work done by the Fish Commission and, quite possibly, the Sportsmen's Club. It is a heavenly stream, with a good population of fish. I caught a very fat brookie, probably the nicest one I've ever taken in Pennsylvania. However, it might well have been a stocker. I also caught some barely legal wild brookies and saw hundreds of wild brook trout parr in some of the springs. Overall, my impression was that this stream is very underrated and deserves a good deal more of my attention.

Campbell Run—4

This little stream, 10 feet wide or less, is heavily abused by cattle. At 63 degrees, it runs cold and has some nice holding water. It is stocked, and I suspect that the only trout I saw was a stocker. I saw no evidence of wild fish.

Church Hill Spring Run—5

This small spring run is a phenomenal TU project waiting to happen. Mossy Creek, a now-famous Trout Unlimited project in Virginia, looked just like this before restoration. This stream is generally about 20 feet wide, the water is 60 degrees in mid-July, and there is all the right weed. This is classic limestone water. The stream is maybe a mile long and would be famous if the cattle could be restrained from mashing its banks. Exclusionary fencing would make it an absolutely first-class fishery, and wild trout would flourish almost immediately. The trout are there—stockers at least—in the relatively few places where there is decent holding water. Both browns and rainbows apparently found their way into this attractive stream, presumably swimming up from the Conococheague when it warmed up. With only two landowners along the stream, this project should be possible. Please, this stream is too good to waste!

Cold Spring Run—6

Another stream that belies its name. With 82-degree water in early August, it is definitely not a trout stream.

Conococheague Creek—7

This fine-looking large stream between Fayetteville and Scotland looked good, but the thermometer indicated thermal problems. The stream is heavily stocked and gets a lot of pressure, which draws attention from other streams in the area. And that is all to the good, but I saw no evidence of any trout (late June), and basically I felt I was in good smallmouth water. (See also South Branch Conococheague Creek, page 137, and West Branch Conococheague Creek, page 139.)

Dennis Creek—8

This small limestoner has nice holding water, all the right weeds, and 64-degree water in mid-July. Only 10 to 20 feet wide, this pretty, stocked stream flows through some quiet meadow stretches where the cattle have not abused it much. The water was up and somewhat off-color when I was there, but at least one stocker brown was interested in my Ausable Wulff. None were interested in my efforts with nymphs—I probably wasn't deep enough. In any event, this is a nice stream and well worth visiting when in the area.

Doylestown Stream—9

This small stream is generally about 6 to 12 feet wide, with occasional larger pools. There is some good holding water, cool temperatures, and trikes in the air. All that is pretty encouraging, but it appears to be freestone, with no signs of trout.

Dry Run—10

This feeder to lovely Spring Run is exceptionally well named—it is dry except during heavy rains. I first tried it right after a rain and found a good deal of cold water. I felt I had made a real discovery, but there were no fish. I did get some stares from the local Amish, and really didn't understand until I returned later and found only a dusty streambed.

East Branch Antietam Creek—11

This really appears to be a freestone stream, although there are some signs of limestone influence in the special-regulation area. The water was cool but certainly not cold. It probably has thermal problems later in the summer. The stocked stream is 20 to 40 feet wide and has nice meanders and gravel in the riffles and nice holding water. However, I couldn't find a fish. In a way that isn't surprising, as there was a lot of good cover where an army of trout could have hidden. It is nice water, but there are better streams in Franklin County.

Falling Spring Branch—12

This is one of the most famous limestone spring creeks in Pennsylvania, and where it is good, it is very good. It's about 20 to 30 feet wide, runs cold (60s in late August), and is famous for its sulphur and *Tricorythodes* hatches. It has all the right aquatic vegetation and a very good head of wild trout. The wild rainbows are famous, but there might be as many browns. Both are gorgeous and look exactly as they should. A few small brookies also turned up, but they might have escaped from a trout nursery.

This stream could be marvelous if some of mankind's "improvements" were removed. Over a mile of stream has been dealt harsh blows, and a substantial section at the lower end has been turned into total junk water. The damage is reversible, but only with time and money. Wouldn't it be great to have the opportunity to build a mile of top-notch fishing water? Wouldn't it have been better to protect it in the first place? The good news is any effort to create new and better habitat is likely to be rewarded with a very healthy population of wild fish.

The Falling Spring Chapter of TU has been involved with the stream for some time now, improving habitat in the upper waters and trying to mitigate the impact of a sewer line. In more recent times they have established a Greenway organization to protect not only the stream and its banks, but also the watershed. This is the only way streams can be reasonably protected.

Devotees claim of the Cumberland Valley limestone streams this is the best water for large trout. True or not, there are plenty of fish here. While the upper water holds wild trout, the lower sections are stocked.

Falls Creek—13

A nice little freestone stream with limestone influence, nice holes, and pocket water, it is about 10 feet wide with a cobbled bottom. Fed by at least one large limestone spring, the stream overall is not particularly frigid. I found the skeleton of a large bluefish (nonnative), which was not an uplifting discovery, but I saw at least one sublegal wild brown, and there are probably others there. A considerable amount of the best holding water was pretty heavily protected by vegetation, and I couldn't get under it with my gear. Nice stream.

Five Forks Creek—14

This is a pretty stream. It is stocked, but I couldn't find any trout. They were either AWOL or laughing at my pitiful attempts. The stream is around 20 feet wide and has nice meanders with plenty of holding water. If it wasn't frigid, it also wasn't steamy. I was surprised that I didn't meet up with any spotted fish here.

Guilford Spring Run—15

This stream is generally unknown because there isn't much to know. Forget this one.

Johnston Run—16

This is a nice stream, with cold water, maybe 15 to 20 feet wide below Mercersburg. There is some aquatic vegetation and meanders with good holding water. Cattle also live along the banks— never a good sign. The only fish I turned up were chubs, which really surprised me. I figured there had to be some trout somewhere, but I couldn't find them.

Later research pointed out that this is yet another stream where a sewer plant has eliminated or greatly reduced the trout population. There is a bright side to the Johnston Run story, however. The treated sewer effluent will be applied on land (sometimes called spray irrigation). The sewer plant discharges will no longer threaten the stream, but instead recharge the groundwater, so more and better springs will be available to keep the stream flowing well. This technique is something our TU chapter has been encouraging for our increasingly urbanized area, and we recommend it to all those interested in protecting their streams. Johnston Run will get another chance, and in a few years it will be a fine trout stream.

Licking Creek—17

Big Spring Creek flows into this meadow stream. It appears Licking Creek is probably ephemeral, as the flow diminished rapidly and there were terrestrial grasses growing in midchannel. It had recently rained a fair amount when I was there, and I'm pretty certain this creek often runs totally dry. I saw no fish.

Little Cove Creek—18

This appears to be a freestone stream in a limestone area. There were a few limestone springs feeding it, but all outward signs said freestone. It is stocked, 15 to 25 feet wide, and flows through neat farms. I heard quail calling back and forth, which is really a rare occurrence these days. There is some nice holding water, but not many trout; the only one I turned up was a stocker. However, the stream and setting are pleasures, even without wild fish.

Markes Run—19

This tiny, 3- to 6-foot-wide limestoner is, in essence, Willow Hill Run, but with cattle. Too many cattle. Even though there is 58-degree water, I didn't see any trout—or much of a place where they could hang out if they were there. The main thing this stream does is give cold water to the Conococheague.

Marsh Run—20

This small limestone spring straddles the Maryland border southwest of Waynesboro. It's about 10 feet wide and 3 feet deep. It has all the attributes of a spring run: watercress growing profusely in the sunny portions, very cold water fed by large springs, and elodea and other aquatic vegetation. It doesn't seem to have any fish. There appears to be some source of contamination, and discovering the cause and correcting the problem might save yet another classic limestone spring run. I ran into a local resident, about thirty years old, who said that in his youth the stream was clogged with so many fish that they could "gig them." This might be a dubious suggestion, but one that certainly indicates something has changed. There just aren't enough limestone spring runs around to allow one to go bad. Part of the problem might be the straddling of the state line. Only a half mile or so of the stream is in Pennsylvania.

Middle Spring Creek (See Cumberland County, Middle Spring Creek, page 119.)—21

Mountain Run—22

This tiny jewel runs frigid right in the village of Scotland. It is only about 6 to 8 feet wide, clear as Wyoming air, and suitably equipped with clean gravel and wild brookies to appreciate it. There isn't a whole lot of great holding water, and it undoubtedly gets heavily fished, but it is a fine little gem.

Muddy Run—23

My first visit to Muddy Run was about midway along the stream, a bit below Route 11, and well below Muddy Run Spring. I found a dry bed and figured that was that. Later I noted the stream was stocked. While the Fish Commission sometimes puts trout in less than ideal habitat in order to disperse early season pressure, I hadn't seen a stocked stream as stressed as this one. Later I returned, went well downstream, and found a fine little limestone creek. It was 10 to 20 feet wide, with wild browns, and with watercress growing along the edges. The water was what might be politely termed as "turbid" when I was there during a heat wave. No rain had fallen for weeks. Cattle were most likely wallowing in the stream to cool off. This seems to be another really nice Franklin County limestoner. Why aren't these streams more evenly spread out so they can be cared for? Anyway, if you are in the area and it hasn't been too hot, give it a try.

Nunnery Run—24

This lovely little spring creek isn't on the maps. It is short, maybe a half mile or so, and it isn't very big, perhaps 6 to 15 feet wide. But it is gorgeous! The major spring that makes the stream rise is near Snow Hill Nunnery cloister, an offshoot of the cloister at Ephrata, site of another engaging spring creek in Lancaster County. The stream runs frigid, with 58-degree water, and has fast riffles and watercress-lined pools. It also has exceptionally picky fish. I was skunked at midday because it was bright. But I went back in the evening and saw a great hatch of cream-colored size 12 mayflies go totally unappreciated. Maybe the fish were stuffed on nymphs. While I remained totally fishless, in the evening I did see enough trout to know they are there. There was a lovely brown of around 19 inches that was not in the slightest bit interested in my clumsy attempts to bring it to hand. Lovely little stream.

Phillaman Run—25

This stream is completely dry.

Red Run—26

This is a good-sized (around 30 feet wide) meadow stream flowing through Amish farms. It is stocked and has just about every desirable type of holding water, limestone outcrops to flow over and create pocket water in, and lots of riffles to produce food. The water was cool—just the way a trout stream should be. The only legal trout I caught was a stocker brown, but I also caught a sublegal, obese rainbow, which from outward appearance was wild. A really fine setting and stream.

Rowe Run—27

This splendid limestone spring creek nearly evaded my search, but a chance conversation with an angler on Green Spring put me onto it. The stream rises from a big spring right at the edge of a limestone belt, and other springs come in along the way to its confluence with Muddy Run near Pinola. It runs about 20 feet wide, but mostly through meadows, and the cattle are not kind to it. In spite of that, there are numerous good holding spots with lots of the right aquatic vegetation. In every sense it's a classic limestoner. It runs cold (59 degrees in June) but not all that clear due to the cattle's influence. There is a good head of fish. The ones I turned up were stockers, both brookies and browns, but they acted like they had some idea what to eat and what to avoid. The cobwebs indicate that sulphurs are an important food source in mid-June, and doubtless there are also other typical forms of insect life present. My standbys—a size 16 Ausable Wulff and a size 14 woven-body stonefly nymph—both produced fish.

If the cattle could be contained, this stream would be as famous as better known spring creeks in Cumberland County. Another TU project awaits.

South Branch Conococheague Creek—28

This small stream flows into the main branch near West Fayetteville. While a number of parts of the Conococheague drainage are pretty neat, this isn't one of them.

Spring Run—29

This fine little limestoner rises in the town of the same name. At its headwaters it is everything a limestone spring run should be: crystal clear, frigid, and loaded with watercress and other aquatic weeds. The bad news is it flows through a meadow with too many cattle, so much of this run's potential is more or less wasted. But, all is not lost. Downstream there are fewer cattle in the meadows and good trout in the stream. These appear to be a combination of wild rainbows, brookies, and other refugees swimming upstream from the Conococheague, as well as some stocked browns. Trikes hatch here, but it is not memorable. I fished this small stream during the height of the cicada hatch of the peak year of 1987. I saw a large bug fall into the stream and immediately get gobbled by a trout, so I whipped a size 8 Ausable Wulff at it, and, whammy, I was into a fine wild rainbow.

This is not a large stream, maybe 10 feet wide in general, and it can't stand a lot of pressure. If those cattle could be contained, it would probably be nationally famous.

Stump Run—30

This stream is virtually dry.

Unnamed Spring Run—31

This tiny spring run appears to be an identical twin to Willow Hill Spring Run. It rises at a large spring in Springtown, is about the same size, is just as brushy, and flows about the same distance into the Conococheague. Here the similarity ends. Someone leased this stream, put signs on every twig and blade of grass warning the public to stay out, and then crammed the thing full of large palominos and rainbows. It's quite possible that these two hatchery types have some redeeming graces, but it is a desecration to take what clearly could be an excellent wild brookie stream and load it down with these.

Welsh Run—32

This small limestoner looks great, feels great, but isn't great. In places it's as narrow as 3 feet, while other places reach up to 10 feet. There is holding water, good cold temperatures, and lots of aquatic vegetation. It looks like it should be loaded with wild fish. But it isn't. Near as I could tell it was barren, a real shame since it appears to have everything needed.

West Branch Antietam Creek—33

Just below the confluence with Five Forks Creek, this stocked stream is sizable, maybe 40 feet wide. There is a lot of aquatic vegetation and seductive currents—the whole bit. However, there appear to be thermal problems, with 71-degree water in mid-June. It is great carp fishing, but the only trout I saw was a brookie dying of what could have been thermal overload. Upstream a bit, at the confluence with Nunnery Run, the stream is narrower and deeper, and it looks as if it was channelized. The water there is cooler, but I still couldn't turn up any trout.

West Branch Conococheague Creek—34

Near Springtown this stocked stream is about 50 feet wide and appears promising. While not in a limestone belt itself, this general area is fed by a number of small limestone spring runs. The water was relatively cool, but I visited during the wet, cold summer of 1989. There was not a lot of great holding water, as cattle have trampled the stream, but there was enough water to expect some trout. They weren't when I was there. I saw loads of chubs, which usually means the absence of a substantial population of wild trout.

Williamson Run—35

This small spring creek appears to be absolutely ideal habitat. It varies between about 6 and 15 feet in width. There are deep holes, flats with seductive slick currents and aquatic vegetation, and bone-chilling water. There are even some prickly pears blooming along the bank. But there were no trout. I couldn't buy a fish. There were a lot of footprints, so some anglers must know something I don't. Everything about this water shouts TROUT, but I can't talk of any.

Willow Brook—36

This is a classic small limestoner, maybe 6 to 10 feet wide. There are loads of watercress and other aquatic vegetation. But the upper sections are posted tight, and the lower section is a trout nursery, so this one can be skipped.

Willow Hill Spring Run—37

This little gem—only 3 to 6 feet wide—rises from a large spring in the town of Willow Hill and flows a short distance to the Conococheague. It is frigid and most of its surface is covered with watercress, with only periodic holes exposing flowing water. It is easy to drive right past it, but if you like native brookies, that would be a mistake! Too small to be an important stream, it nevertheless appears to have a nice population of fat wild brookies. It really does deserve special mention—and protection.

I had a heart-stopping experience while fishing along this tiny jewel. While creeping up the bank, looking for room to cast, I managed to step on top of a very protective hen mallard doing her best to shelter her brood of ducklings from my intrusion. For the next few seconds I thought I had stepped on a feathered landmine: noise, astonishment, and critters flapping in all directions. It took me a while to gather my composure and press on. If you get a kick out of brushy little streams, which at times I do, keep this one in mind, but watch out for the hen mallard!

Wilson Run—38

This stream is sort of a junior varsity Dennis Creek. It is a bit smaller, a bit warmer (but with 65-degree water, not at all bad for mid-July), and has a cobbled bottom and nice holding water. The mystery is that no fish showed up. Perhaps the most important thing about this small stream is that Joseph Armstrong settled there in 1737. I don't know if he was a relative, but most people with this name were chased out of Scotland, and it is possible we both wear the same tartan.

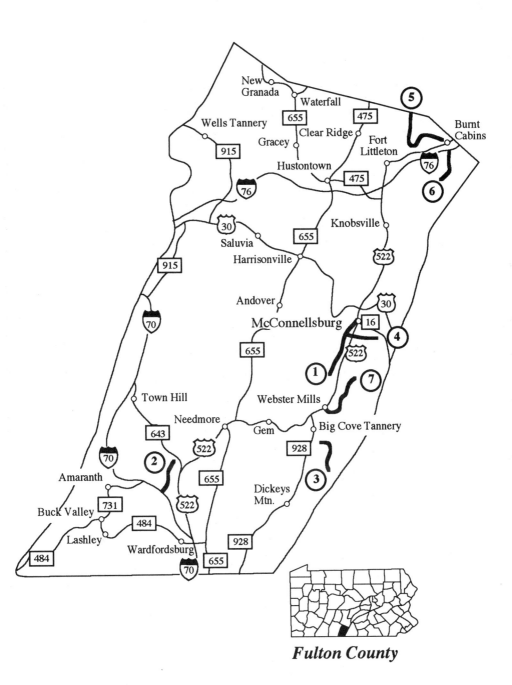

Fulton County

FULTON COUNTY

First glance shows that Fulton County is bounded by Bedford, Franklin, and Huntingdon counties, all prime areas for limestone waters in Pennsylvania. This would indicate that Fulton County is also a top area. Unfortunately, this is not the case. It isn't a disaster, but it isn't near the top of the list either.

It is pretty, pastoral, and a pleasant area to visit. Esther Run, Spring Run, and Cove Creek are clearly limestone waters and have a good deal to recommend them. However (and it's tough to complain about this), there are so many really good areas for limestone stream fishing in the Commonwealth that this area just doesn't make the cut. If thunderstorms blow away plans for one of the nearby counties, then Fulton County could be an alternative. The streams probably won't be crowded, especially after early season.

Cove Creek—1

I was at Cove Creek at its confluence with Spring Run after heavy rains, and it was badly discolored. It appeared to be a stocked, freestone stream with no obvious characteristics of a limestone water. Later I went upstream, near Rock Hill Road, and found what was clearly limestone water, with rich farms, too many cows, and a considerable amount of very impressive restoration work. The water temperature was in the mid-60s. No doubt there are trout here, but all I turned up were chubs and a number of carp going through their spawning rituals.

Cove Run—2

This is a miniature limestoner, with good cold water and limestone ledges for the stream to bubble over. However, it is only 3 to 5 feet wide, and while there are probably some trout in there, this is only for the small-stream fanatic.

Esther Run—3

This surprising stream is about 20 feet wide and looks like another freestone stream, with lots of rocks, runs, miniature pocket water, and pools and riffles. It also has very cold water (a very unusual 57 degrees in mid-July). To further add to the unusual qualities, there was a myriad of what appeared to be wild rainbows. I turned them up in two year classes, and there seemed to be a young of the year next to every rock in the stream. My visit was cut short by a deluge. A very unusual stream, it is a nice one to fish.

Kendall Creek—4

This small limestoner is probably too little to interest anyone other than the small-stream aficionado. At 3 to 6 feet wide, much of that covered with overhanging vegetation, there isn't much fishing water. In addition, when I was there it ran muddy, presumably the contribution of some cattle, as it was a dry time. It also ran quite cold at 60 degrees in mid-July. No trout turned up, but there are probably some there. It had all the characteristics of limestone water. Too bad it isn't larger.

Little Aughwick Creek—5

This sizable stream seemed to be ideal smallmouth water. The temperature, 75 degrees at 10 o'clock on an August morning, was too hot for trout, but if smallmouths are your game, go and learn more about this stocked stream.

South Branch Little Aughwick Creek—6

This medium-sized, stocked stream (20 to 30 feet wide) looked better than it turned out to be. It featured decent holding water and a good population of chubs a short distance below Burnt Cabins. The water was 70 degrees, which for early August was an encouraging sign. While it had all the appearances of a freestone stream, it was not badly dewatered. In general it appeared to be an attractive body of water, with everything ideal for trout. But I couldn't turn up any at all. Maybe with a little more perseverance, I might have pounded up a stocker or two.

Spring Run—7

I was on this fine small stream below Websters Mills, where it is around 15 feet wide. It has pleasant pools and riffles, with a reasonable number of undercut banks and overhanging sycamore trees, and 60-degree water. There is aquatic vegetation swaying in the current. In general, it appears to be a nice little limestone stream in charming pastoral country of old farms reminiscent of the west of Scotland. But I might not have done the fishing justice. The only fish I caught, or saw others catch, were stocker rainbows. No one I spoke with indicated any knowledge of wild fish in the stream, which is a pity. It's a pretty stream, but not memorable from a fisher's point of view.

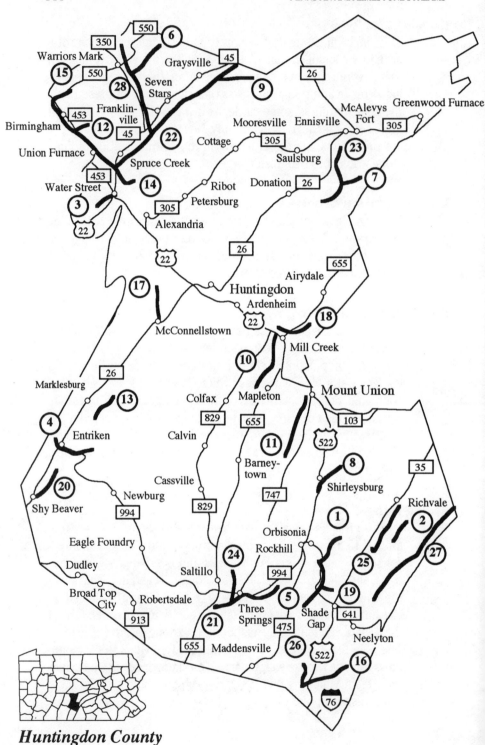

Huntingdon County

HUNTINGDON COUNTY

This is one of the major areas for limestone fishing in the Commonwealth. While it is overshadowed to some extent by the enormous concentration of superb waters in Centre County, it can certainly hold its own with any area as far as its best streams are concerned.

Spruce Creek is clearly the diamond in the crown. It is a magnificent stream, famous as fishing water for several presidents. With exquisite wild browns and a few brookies, it is quintessential limestone water. It ranks high on anyone's list of best waters not only in the state but also the country. The down side is the number of signs suggesting that whatever it is you want to do can best be done elsewhere.

The Little Juniata can justly claim to be a limestoner and it might be the largest one, although Penns Creek is a challenger. I would be hard-pressed to choose which is larger. In spite of devastating fish-kills, the Little Juniata just bounces right back. It has a great population of trout, both wild and planted as fingerlings. Rumor has it there are fish as long as your leg in the deep holes. It also has great insect hatches.

There are lots of other, smaller, great little limestone streams squirreled away in various nooks and crannies of the county, and they are worthwhile if small streams are your thing or if rains roil the larger waters. Logan Spring Run, Warriors Mark Run, and Trough Spring Creek all fit this description.

No effort at thorough coverage of Pennsylvania limestone fishing can exclude Huntingdon County and its two major and several minor limestone streams. This is central Pennsylvania in the true sense: fine scenery, fine water, and fine wild trout.

Blacklog Creek—1

This is a substantial stream, maybe 35 or 40 feet wide near its confluence with Shade Creek. I tried several times before I could fish the stocked water under decent conditions. In early season it was full, almost voluptuous looking. I went away thinking I had found real treasure—which the angling world had unaccountably overlooked. When I returned in August, the promising runs of May had turned out to be populated by carp, and the stream was warm, low, muddy, and totally uninviting. What a disappointment!

Blocks Run—2

This stream was dry in early August. Since that is a stressful environment for most trout, I did not tarry.

Canoe Valley Run—3

A nice little stream around 10 feet wide with frigid water (57 degrees)—and some nasty problems. The good folks of Water Street have found a cheap solution to their solid-waste problems: they simply throw their trash into this neat little stream. From the amount of filamentous algae in parts of the stream, there is probably more than trash involved. The algae and festoons of plastic do nothing for the aesthetics. But in spite of the outrageous behavior of the locals, there is a good population of wild browns.

Coffee Run—4

This is a tiny trickle, but at least the water is cold (68 degrees). While it is quite possible there are some trout somewhere along it, there seems no feasible way to fish it. Pulling the overhanging grass away to open up a spot to get a lure into the water would spook all the fish—if they are there. Not a fishery, in my opinion.

What does a real fisherman have to say? Frank Nale, who can probably catch trout in most parking lots, said he managed to extract two browns in the 16-inch range from this tiny stream. But he did at least allow that it wouldn't appeal to most people.

Craig Run—5

Bone dry in early August.

Dry Run—6

Unlike the other streams with the same name in the state, this one has water in it! However, it is small, warm, and trampled by cattle. Not trout water.

East Branch Standing Stone Creek—7

This is a stocked stream, maybe 15 to 20 feet wide, with some holding water and cool temperatures. However, it may not have been due to limestone springs, since the weather was also cool. I caught loads of chubs and scared out a stocker-sized trout. My hunch is this is a freestone stream, and for me not a memorable one either way. Nevertheless, Frank Nale turned up a number of trout, both stocked and wild. They were mostly browns, but there was at least one sublegal brookie.

Fort Run—8

This small stream—about 10 feet wide—was a disappointment. It ran cool with 67-degree water in early August and had good holding water and nice riffles with loads of life under the rocks. In short, it looked ideal for native brookies, so I was surprised I saw none. It's not a major stream, but it appeared to have everything needed for a wild trout population. This stream is worth trying if other, more prominent waters are muddied up.

Fowler Run—9

This is a true limestone stream. Unfortunately, it is so small it can't be considered a fishery.

Hares Valley Creek—10

A wide, shallow little stream, maybe 30 feet wide and 3 inches deep. Air and water temperatures were the same. From all signs this is a freestone stream. It would be chub water except it is too shallow.

Hill Valley Creek—11

This stream appears to be a limestone creek, but it is very small. Water temperature in early August was 71 degrees. While there seemed to be a decent amount of water, there was very little holding water and no trout. It is not in any way an exciting stream.

Hundred Springs—12

This is one of the few limestone lakes in the Commonwealth. There is a short, frigid stream entering the lake, and a short, much warmer stream exiting. There are probably a hundred springs, most of which have been dammed by a water company. Apparently there are loads of springs in the bottom of the impoundment as well. There are trout in evidence swimming around. I have no idea what the deal is on fishing there, but there are no signs requesting people to stay away.

James Creek—13

This stream has cold enough water (68 degrees) to be interesting,

but there isn't enough of it. There might be a trout or two squirreled away somewhere, but the stream is tiny (the grass from
each shore crosses in midstream).

Little Juniata River (See Blair County, Little Juniata River, page 72.)—14

Logan Spring Run—15

This is one of those tiny jewels that we all wish were ten times
larger. If it were, it would be known all over the country. It really
is small—maybe 3 feet wide in places, maybe 7 feet wide in other
places—but it is all limestone spring creek, just in miniature.
There are some lovely wild browns there, nothing huge due to the
holding-water constraints, but maybe up to 10 inches or so. Wher-
ever there is enough holding water to prevent sunburned backs,
there are trout.

Mark Nale reports that local rumor has it that numbers of
Little Juniata fish will move into this stream if low-water/high-tem-
perature problems afflict that water.

North Branch Aughwick Creek—16

I was on this medium-sized, stocked stream near its confluence
with Trout Run, a short distance north of Burnt Cabins. The
stream is about 25 feet wide but had very little flow and gave all
the indications of being a freestone stream. Aside from a good
number of wood ducks, I saw nothing much of interest. Not good
trout water.

North Branch Crooked Creek—17

This is a typical freestone stream in its headwaters, but it picks up
a good jolt of cold, nutrient-laden water around McConnellstown,
where the stream was 64 degrees in late August. However, the cold
water warms up fast. The stream is around 10 to 15 feet wide.
There are a good number of trout, which I managed to scare out of
a few years' growth but not to catch. They all appeared to be stocker size, so they probably are just that—stockers. There is a substantial impounded spring in town with some equally substantial
trout gliding around in it. Frank Nale indicated that he turns up
wild trout, including some good-sized ones. This is definitely a
limestone stream (it flows through a quarry!), but a minor one.

Saddler Creek—18

This pretty, stocked stream appears to be freestone, with lots of small waterfalls over shale outcrops. There are some substantial springs that dump what appears to be limestone water into it; however, the overall impression is of a freestone stream, and a very pretty one. The only trout I tangled with was at one of the spring feeders, and I lost that fish so I can't say whether it was a wild fish or one of the stockers. I do know it was a brown. Overall, the stream is pretty and no doubt worth some attention if you're in the neighborhood. Not worth a special trip.

Shade Creek—19

While there is at least one major limestone quarry adjacent to this stream, it has all the earmarks of a freestoner. Early in the year it is a good-sized stream, maybe 30 feet or more wide, but it really loses water in midsummer. When I went back during low-water conditions, many riffles were exposed stone, with the water gurgling out of sight below. I did catch some stocker browns, which not surprisingly held in the deeper pools. No sign of wild fish, though. It must be a marginal stream due to the low water.

Shy Beaver Creek—20

What a sensational name! What a totally barren stream. The tragedy of this stream is that it is dry. This was one of the places that I had been eagerly looking forward to visiting, because of its great name. Alas, it was not meant to be. Enjoy the name, but don't bother to check it out.

Spring Creek—21

This is a very promising name for a limestone stream; unfortunately, it doesn't come within a mile of its more famous namesakes. It is a tiny trickle.

Spruce Creek (See also Spruce Creek, Centre County, page 93.)—22

Presidents have often been guests at one or another of the clubs along this famous stream. I had one occasion to fish the Spruce Creek Rod and Gun Club water. It is a spectacular section of limestone stream, but for whatever reason, they have put a lot of stockers on top of good wild fish. The stream itself is a marvel. It is loaded with just about any insect you can imagine and also loaded with wild browns that grow to prodigious size. Unfortunately, for the average guy it is also loaded with signs suggesting he take his business elsewhere. The Penn State section is a short piece of nice water in the midst of a sign seller's dream. Fishing with restrictions is allowed in this nice water, which boasts a healthy population of wild brown trout. It isn't heavenly water, but it is worth your time. Above and below this section are areas posted with signs suggesting anything but come on in. It would be great to have more available water on this famous stream.

It is worth quoting Frank Nale directly on this one, as what he has to say is so astonishing that I don't want to be accused of embellishing anything:

"This stream ranks number thirteen on my all-time-best-stream list. I've caught 428 trout there since 1983, though I didn't fish it in 1984 or 1985 and only once in 1983. In 1989 I fished there five times and caught 136 trout at an average rate of 11.1 per hour. My best day yielded 55. In 1986 I fished it seven times and caught 109 trout at a rate of 11.61 per hour. Best day yielded 60. Almost all of my fishing was done in the Penn State stretch. This section has a water-temperature problem, and I wouldn't recommend fishing it in the evening after a hot summer day or two, unless of course the water level is higher than normal for some reason.

"If no one else is fishing there, which is rare, it's rather easy to catch 20 trout per hour. Most of the trout are wild browns except now and then a stockie can be caught. They average maybe 9 inches, though I've caught four trout here over 16 inches. I believe these four were all stockies."

Standing Stone Creek—23

Above Jackson Corner, where I was, this is a substantial, stocked stream, maybe 50 feet wide. While the water was pretty cool, so was the air. It really looked like a nice freestone smallmouth stream. There were loads of chubs but no trout.

The Nale brothers, Mark and Frank, add that they also fished it, farther upstream above McAlevys Fort, and turned up a total of ten browns and two brookies in a bit over three hours. They indicated that it certainly appeared to be a freestoner in that stretch.

Three Springs Creek—24

This stream might be a limestoner, but for me it's not a memorable one. It is warm, loaded with chubs, and has a world-class population of crawfish. It's supposed to be stocked, but I saw no sign of any trout. I couldn't find the three springs, either.

Trough Spring Creek—25

I can't say for sure whether this nice little stream is a limestoner or not. It's about 5 to 10 feet wide and in places has some aquatic weed. The water temperature was 70 degrees on a very hot, humid day. I started off downstream and immediately discovered a convention of wood ducks, which had spooked the fish for a long distance. So I decided to try upstream. The pastured cattle had not been kind to the stream, but it was not obliterated. I scared a number of what I felt were trout before connecting (with an Ausable Wulff naturally) with a fine wild brookie of about 10 inches. I then went back downstream and looked over some of what I had terrified earlier, and in a number of cases saw white-tipped fins under obstructions. It's not a fantastic population of wild brookies, but for someone more careful than I was that day, it could be a fun little stream to fish.

Trout Run—26

This tiny—generally less than 10 feet wide—feeder to the North Branch of Aughwick Creek appears to be a freestone stream. It was very low in early August when I was there, and it wasn't particularly cold (71 degrees in the morning). No signs of trout, not even any decent-sized chubs. It is possible that well up in the headwaters there might be a small brookie population, but in general Trout Run is just one more forgettable stream.

Tuscarora Creek—27

This stream is not a limestone stream. It is stocked, and it has what must be the greatest population of crawfish in the entire world. While that may be very valuable information for smallmouth fishermen or someone anxious to take a crack at Cajun cooking, neither were high on my list right then, so I continued on my way.

Warriors Mark Run—28

This is a true limestone stream, and it has a good population of

wild brown trout. Unfortunately, the population of "No Trespassing" signs is even higher. Nevertheless, there is a short section
down near the confluence with Spruce Creek where the signs
aren't in evidence and the wild browns are. Although not a truly
great one, it is a good stream—a real treasure. I hope the people
who pay for the leases and signs are also paying to take care of
their stream. This stream was damaged a few years ago by a pile
of manure, which wiped out most of the stream as well as good
portions of Spruce Creek.

Mark Nale advises that this is a classic and very productive
limestoner. While most of the water is posted, he manages to have
some access to the stream and catches prodigious numbers of
wild browns to about 16 inches. He says that on his last visit he
picked up seventeen fish. Apparently there are good numbers of
browns in the 12- to 14-inch range in the limestone portion of the
stream, which begins a half mile above the village of Warriors
Mark. Good stream, and worth visiting if you can wangle an invitation!

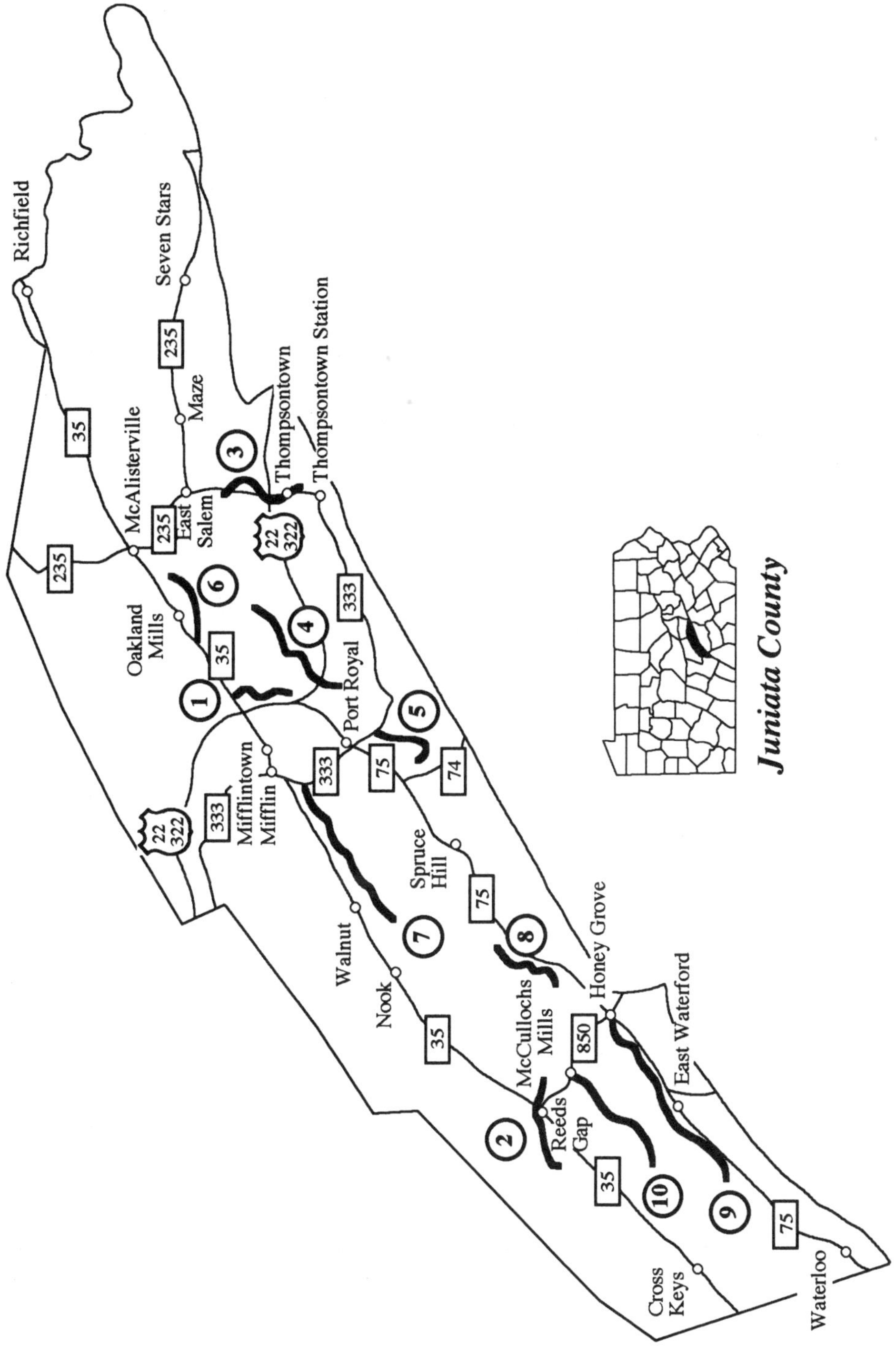

Richfield

Seven Stars

235

Maze

McAlisterville

35

Thompsontown

Thompsontown Station

235

East Salem

22 322

235

③

Oakland Mills

⑥

333

④

35

①

Port Royal

⑤

333

75

22 322

333

74

Mifflintown

Mifflin

Walnut

333

Spruce Hill

⑦

75

Nook

75

⑧

35

Honey Grove

McCullochs Mills

East Waterford

850

②

Reeds Gap

35

⑩

⑨

75

Cross Keys

Waterloo

Juniata County

JUNIATA COUNTY

Central Pennsylvania is famous for the quality of its many limestone streams, and Juniata County is about as central as it's possible to be in Pennsylvania—but the limestone largely passed this area by.

The best streams appear to be largely freestone, with Willow Run and its feeder Daugherty Run leading the parade. Delaware Creek is a nice little stream that runs frigid in midsummer and has some wild browns along with a number of stockers that are still in great shape late in the season.

It isn't that Juniata County is a bad place to fish, it's just that there are so many better places around it that it's tough to justify spending a lot of time there. However, if big water and big toothy fish are your thing, then fish the county's namesake river, but not for trout.

Cedar Spring—1

This stream is tiny and very brushy. It has cool but not frigid water. It is possible that there are a few trout in it, but I couldn't find anyplace to get a fly into the water—and I'm willing to fish some pretty small water.

Daugherty Run—2

This nice little stream is below Reeds Gap. It's 10 to 15 feet wide and a thoroughly pleasant little stream. With temperatures in the low 70s, the water was cool enough to be of interest; however, there is minimal limestone influence. I saw a few small wild browns and there were probably other, better ones I couldn't entice. It makes sense that there would be wild browns here, as this feeds Willow Run, which is freestone but is first-class wild trout water.

Delaware Creek—3

This is a really good, stocked stream. It varies widely in size from around 20 feet down to maybe 5 feet in places. It is fed by a large spring a few miles above Route 322, which gives it frigid water and a distinctive limestone style. I was run out by a thunderstorm, but not before I had a chance to sample some of what is in the stream. There are nice brookies, which are probably stockers, and also a good number of browns, which appear to be wild. At 61 degrees, there is very nice holding water, parts with meanders and pools and other parts with pocket water under the hemlocks. I wonder how many people (including me) drive over this stream on their way to much more famous streams. This is not a large stream, and it can't take major pressure, but it is a good honest stream in seemingly ideal habitat, with good numbers of trout. I wish we had a stream like it close to home.

Doe Run—4

This stream is about 20 feet wide at the town of Mexico, and it has thermal problems. Above Mexico the water temperature was 82 degrees, so it's of no interest to trout fishers. However, in town the temperature was down to 77 degrees, so there may be a few refugees that came up from the Juniata. I couldn't find them, though.

Hunters Creek—5

This is a nice enough little stream, maybe 10 to 15 feet wide above Old Port, where it must pick up some seeps as the water temperature gets down to 74 degrees. However, I couldn't find any evidence of trout, although a few probably hole up there in summer. It's another forgettable stream.

Little Lost Creek—6

This stream has been demolished by cattle. With 86-degree water, it holds little interest to trout fishers.

Markee Creek—7

This small stream had 76-degree water when the air was only 75 degrees. While it is in a limestone belt, it appeared to be freestone in every way. There was no evidence of any trout in the stream.

Path Creek—8

This is a real nothing stream. It is only about 3 to 5 feet wide, and it had 81-degree water when the air was 79 degrees. Not trout water!

Tuscarora Creek—9

This substantial stream is wide and shallow and is not trout water. It does have some very deep holes, but with 84-degree water it's of more interest to smallmouth and muskie fishermen than to trout fishermen. There is some stocking above Perulack, but with these temperatures they were long gone by the time I was there in midsummer.

Willow Run—10

This small stream—maybe 10 feet or so wide—is reputed to hold a considerable number of sizable brown trout. While I did turn up a nice holdover brown of maybe 13 inches, I did not see much evidence of limestone influence.

Don Douple advises that the stream looks like limestone water up near its source (above where I was) and is "silent" water—that is, no riffles, very brushy, very difficult to approach the fish, and generally tough fishing. Might be why there are decent numbers of wild browns!

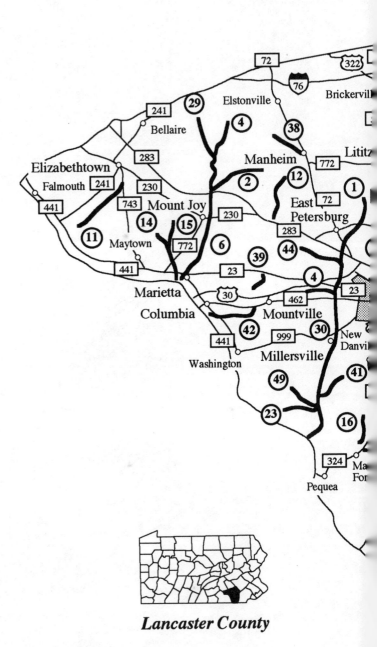

Lancaster County

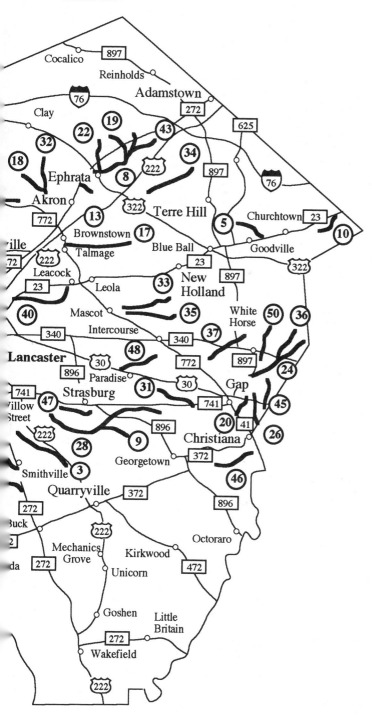

LANCASTER COUNTY

There is no question that this is a scenic area. In the eastern part of the county the Amish and Mennonite farmers are famous. There is a cost for their agricultural practices. The streams of the area run muddy throughout the year and warm in summer.

As for the limestoners, Lancaster County leads the list in number, but it ranks very near the bottom for quality. The vast majority appear to be beyond quick recovery. While streams can make rapid recoveries when the cause of the problem is removed, many of the promising streams here do not seem destined to return to health any time soon.

It's not fair, however, to point the finger at the farmers and wish them ill. We should be able to work out a system to allow these good people to earn a decent living without destroying a key part of the environment.

George Myers, who has fished Lancaster County streams for about forty-five years and is a long-time active TU member, said he wasn't very familiar with the streams I had visited, although he knew of a few neat non-limestone streams in the county, including some with wild brookies and browns. The message is pretty clear: if you want good fishing, get away from those productive limestone belts, which is just the opposite from advice for most parts of Pennsylvania.

This is not to say that there isn't good fishing—or nice limestone streams—in Lancaster County. Donegal Spring Creek must be the best limestoner in the county, and it is a nice stream that has received many hours of stream restoration work. Indian Run is mainly of interest because it is an honest-to-gosh spring creek right near Ephrata, while Cedar Creek is the same in the Amish country. Lititz Run could be a splendid stream if another means of handling sewage could be devised. A number of other streams seem to have possibilities, but for now the problems appear large and insurmountable.

Bachman Run—1
My notes seem to sum it up: 82-degree water, a nothing stream.

Back Run—2
Simply put, 87-degree water can be harmful to the health of trout.

Big Beaver Creek—3
This is pretty much a bookend to Little Beaver Creek. By the time

I got there the water was 86 degrees and the stocked trout were long gone.

Brubaker Run—4

Eighty-six-degree water is definitely enough to wreck the day for a trout.

Cedar Creek—5

This is a spring creek surviving in the middle of the Amish country. Well sort of surviving. I couldn't see any evidence of trout, although there appeared to be fine holding water and lots of aquatic vegetation and cool water (72 degrees). At 15 feet wide, it isn't reminiscent of Penns Creek; but it certainly appears to have good things going for it. The meadow sections have not been pounded flat by cattle or draft horses, and in general it looks fine. But I couldn't turn up any trout. Nice stream with a definite future.

Chickies Creek—6

I fished this stream at the confluence with Dellinger Run. It was smallmouth water, or possibly even carp water, with 78-degree water and no sign of any suitable trout habitat.

Climbers Run—7

This small stream has been pretty heavily damaged by cattle. It is around 10 feet wide near its lower end, where it is stocked. In spite of hot weather the water temperature was 74 degrees and there was some nice holding water, but I couldn't turn up anything interesting. I have heard persistent rumors that in the upper reaches, which aren't in a limestone area, there are wild trout. That would be great, as there are precious few in Lancaster County.

Cocalico Creek—8

The only serious difference between this and Harnish Run is that I was below Reamstown. Another wiped-out stream.

Colamus Run—9

This stream is only about a foot wide! Sometimes there is very nice fishing in small streams, but not here.

Conestoga Creek—10

Near Morgantown this stream runs through a limestone belt. With 81-degree water in the morning, any trout must be long gone by late July. The carp, however, are there in numbers.

Conoy Creek—11

This is a nice-sized, stocked stream, about 25 to 30 feet wide where I was (near Trout Run Road). It was badly dewatered in early August, and the water temperature of 75 was marginal. The stream appeared to be freestone, although the rock outcrops were limestone. There were a number of chubs but no sign of any trout. That applied as well for Trout Run, which turned out to be only a promising name. Overall there wasn't much decent holding water and, apparently, no trout.

Dellinger Run—12

This "stream" was dry in early August.

Diamond Spring—13

It may be that most of the output of the spring is now bottled for sale as ersatz Perrier water. The long and short of it is that the stream is virtually dry.

Donegal Creek—14

This is the sister stream of Donegal Spring Creek, and a poor relative at that. It is badly trampled by cattle and not very inviting. Where I was, near the confluence of the two streams, Donegal Creek ran about 78 degrees, while nearby Donegal Spring Creek ran substantially cooler. It is doubtful that trout (even the stockers) would hold in Donegal Creek with the nearby colder spring water available.

Donegal Spring Creek—15

This appears to be an important stream! If it were in Centre County, it would not merit much attention, but in Lancaster County, with its abused streams, this one stands out. It's about 25 to 35 feet wide, seems to have the right hatches, and maintains cool temperatures through the summer. There has been a massive amount of work done on the stream, some of it not overly aesthetic (which remains one of the dilemmas of stream restoration efforts), but the net effect is positive. There are good numbers of fish, and among the stockers are wild fish. I turned up some wild browns, including one sublegal, and also caught what appeared to be a wild rainbow, a rarity in the state. The special-regulation area gets a good deal of attention, but with the number of fish holding through the year, most fish probably are returned to fight again another day.

It's a pretty stream in an engaging pastoral setting. There are good numbers of freely rising fish that clearly have enough surface activity to keep them happy. This stream deserves a better review than history has given it. It is not a classic limestone spring run, as it has riffles, pools, and meanders, but it's a nice place to fish. This stream offers rural surroundings, plenty of rising fish, and the chance to see other wildlife. I saw a fox and a hawk, which took a swipe at some ducks I had flushed. I fished this stream several times during the summer and found each stop well worth it. Put this one on the list of worthwhile streams.

Goods Run—16

Nice-looking small stream of about 10 to 15 feet wide. In the midst of very hot weather the water temperature was 74 degrees, which isn't bad at all. Some nice holding water, lots of minnows, but no decent-sized fish, not even chubs. Why? The problem is probably silt, which is plentiful.

Graff Creek—17

I was there on a hot, humid day. The stream was 86 degrees with 90-degree air temperatures. Enough said.

Hammer Creek—18

I found out a long time ago that 86-degree water is definitely bad for the health of stocked trout, so I kept on going. (See also Hammer Creek, Lebanon County, page 171.)

Harnish Run—19

Where I was, a bit above Reamstown, the water was 86 degrees. I didn't inquire further.

Houston Run—20

This is a nice little stream in spite of the destructive habits of cattle. It has some large springs that keep it pleasantly cool. With some tender loving care it could really be a lovely fishery.

Huber Run—21
This stream is just too small to be of interest to trout fishermen.

Indian Run I—22
What a totally unexpected pleasure to come upon this lovely limestone spring creek. It is practically everything a spring creek should be: cold, with loads of watercress and elodea, low gradient, smooth surface, and loads of sow bugs. The bad news is that the only trout I caught—in late August—was a splendid brookie that looked like a stocker. It might be possible to get some wild fish established here. There are some cattle problems, and the spring run section above Ephrata where it flows into the Cocalico Creek is short, just a mile or two long, but substantial springs form the creek at Springville. For those who love to fish classic limestone water and don't want to drive farther, this is a good-looking stream in an attractive setting. It would be great to have wild fish in it, a worthy TU project.

Indian Run II—23
This small feeder to the Little Conestoga, near Rock Hill, had 82-degree water. Not trout water!

Indian Spring Run—24
This stream is tiny and not really a trout fishery. There are persistent rumors of a remnant native brookie population in the uppermost sections, but this may be above the limestone section.

Landis Run—25
Ninety-degree, hot, humid air produced 87-degree water in this tiny, forgettable stream.

Limeville Run—26
With 86-degree water, this stream is terminal at this point.

Lititz Run—27
This beautiful little limestoner runs right through the town of Lititz and keeps cold water for some distance below. It is a typi-

cal limestone stream in a likable area, with loads of swaying aquatic vegetation in low-gradient sections and some pools and riffles in other sections. The good news is the stream is stocked by a local sportsmen's club. The bad news is that just below Lititz is a sewer plant. I can't say there are no trout below the plant's discharge point, but I can say I didn't see any sign of any, despite the very trouty-looking water. There were *Tricorythodes* in the air and on the water, but no trout. Given all the damaged streams in Lancaster County, I was really disappointed. I felt I had stumbled onto a gem, but it appears to be a dirty and mistreated body of water. I hope something can be done to bring it back.

Little Beaver Creek—28

This pretty, stocked stream has the same malaise as many other Lancaster County streams: warm, dirty water. At 85 degrees the water is a bit cooler than a number of nearby streams, but it is clearly too warm for trout.

Little Chickies Creek—29

At Rissers Mill this nice stream is about 25 feet wide, but it had 81-degree water in early August. There was a very cold (56 degrees) small spring run nearby, but no sign of the stocked trout either in the small run or in the confluence with Little Chickies Creek.

Little Conestoga Creek—30

While this is a stocked stream, it had 88-degree water when I measured it. So, besides spreading out some opening-day pressures, this one can be avoided.

Londonland Run—31

This is one of the many eastern Lancaster County streams that have been obliterated by local agricultural practices. It's possible that it can be revived, but it is hard to convince a midsummer visitor of that. It is stocked, but this must be to distribute opening-day pressure. With 86-degree water in mid-July the stream has very little going for it.

Middle Creek—32

I was on the stream near the confluence with Hammer Creek.

With 83-degree water in Middle Creek, it represents a trout desert (although it's supposed to be stocked).

Mill Creek—33

Yet another in the seemingly endless list of badly abused Lancaster County limestone streams. This one had 90-degree water.

Muddy Creek—34

This substantial creek is maybe 60 to 70 feet wide, slow moving, and muddy (imagine that). It is also pretty warm. Even in the cold, rainy summer of 1989 when I was there, the water ran between 76 and 78 degrees. This is not trout water, but it might be quite good carp water.

Muddy Run—35

This well-named stream sported 92-degree water when I was there. End of discussion.

Pequea Creek—36

This impoverished stream is a classic example of what is sometimes needed to spread out opening-day pressures. Any decent holding water has been more or less wiped out by cattle mauling the banks. However, if stalking opening-day stockers is your thing, then this is your stream!

Richardson Run—37

This badly abused stream had 88-degree water on a late July afternoon. It is a shame, but perhaps its future is better than its present.

Rife Run—38

At Manheim this stream had 92-degree water. On to the next one.

Silver Spring—39

Eighty-seven-degree water definitely discourages trout!

Stauffer Run—40

Most trout don't do well in 84-degree water. Perhaps one day we will figure out how to use redband trout genes to breed brookies so we can release them into warm water. Until then, don't check out Stauffer Run.

Stehman Run—41

This is a nice little stream where I saw it at Rock Hill, but the water, at 76 degrees, would stress any trout. (Not that I saw any!)

Stickler Run—42

This small limestone stream runs through the edge of the town of Columbia, but apparently not the right side of town from the look of things. It has nice holding water, and with 73-degree water it is within the tolerable range for trout. There is some very toothsome-looking pocket water and pools and riffles farther upstream, along with a lot of junk—mostly bits and pieces of wrecked automobiles dropped down the steep bank. What a shame to waste such good habitat. No trout are in evidence, and I don't blame them. The aesthetics are appalling. The stream is waiting for a TU chapter. With a good deal of cleanup, it would probably make a good home for browns, and adding another wild trout stream is certainly worthwhile!

Stony Run—43

This stream is too small for even me to fish, and that's small! I doubt if anyone would find it appealing.

Swarr Run—44

At 5 to 15 feet wide, there are larger streams and colder water, but this nice little stream is stocked and appears to have the necessary habitat for holding fish through the summer. But I didn't turn up any of the stockers in spite of the help of some great exclusionary fencing to keep cattle away from the stream.

Umblestown Run—45

This stream is tiny. Not a trout fishery in any normal sense.

Valley Run—46

This small stream is the twin to the Atglen Valley Creek in western Chester County. It is equally warm and, from a trout's point of view, unappealing. It is not trout water.

Walnut Run—47

A small, abused stream running through lovely farmland. With 86-

degree water the possibilities of trout are a bit lean. Enjoy the scenery and leave the rod in the case.

Watsons Run—48

This badly abused stream is tiny, too small to be a trout fishery. The neighboring streams also have been abused, possibly beyond reclaiming.

West Branch Little Conestoga Creek—49

This pleasant-looking stream is better to look at than to fish. With 79-degree water it is stocked but of little interest to trout fishermen.

White Horse Run—50

This is a nice stream, and it should have trout in it. It is around 20 feet wide, and in spite of the best efforts of many trampling cattle, the stream more or less looks like a stream. There are a number of substantial springs pumping good, cold water into it. In mid-August of 1988 the water was running 71 degrees. There is good vegetation, nice holding water, and apparently everything but trout. This stream is worth some attention, as it is potentially a real fishery in an area that is largely wasteland.

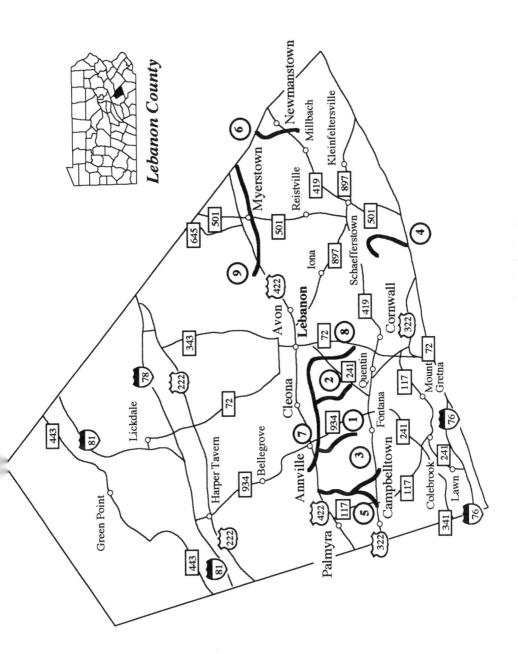

Lebanon County

LEBANON COUNTY

This relatively small county has some handsome spring creeks, which seem to have escaped notice. Bachman Run, Killinger Creek, and Beck Creek are all classic limestoners. The Upper Tulpehocken is here and is a classic limestoner also, but parts are heavily posted.

This is a place to go for a change. A trip here is a trip back in time, to fine country, well-tended farms, less-hurried days, traditional values, and an air of prosperity. Some suburbanization is creeping in, and, frankly, the fishing isn't as good as in some other limestone areas. But the experience is much more satisfying than the fishing—worth the trip.

Bachman Run—1

This stream is a larger version—about twice the width at 15 to 20 feet—of Killinger Creek, which it parallels at a discreet distance. Cattle have trampled the banks, leaving little good holding water. There are numerous signs of stream restoration work, done some time ago and now in need of repair. The stream runs cold, and there are midsummer *Tricorythodes* and Blue-winged Olive hatches. It is a stocked stream and appears to hold only stocked fish. I didn't turn up anything that I could consider wild, but on the other hand, the stockers, both brooks and browns, were very nice fish. The browns ran to 14 inches and the brookies to 12 inches—fine, broad-shouldered fish that fought well. A fine little stream as is, it could be made even better.

Beck Creek—2

This is a simply gorgeous low-gradient limestoner. Fed by large springs, it runs frigid all summer long. It has loads of watercress fringes, with other aquatic weed swaying in gentle currents. And like many streams below a golf course, the bottom is peppered with golf balls. I figured that water this good-looking had to have large numbers of wild browns, but it doesn't appear to. Much of the nicest water is leased by the Susquehannock Fly Fishers, who have put up signs suggesting that entering that land might be about as much fun as entering a minefield. So, although it looked like delectable water, I didn't try it.

The downstream section is an interesting-looking meadow stretch, with lots of overhanging grasses and an impressive grasshopper population. With all that beautiful cold water, I thought there had to be some action. I went down as far as Quittapahilla Creek and then started back up. I managed to chase some ducks ahead of me, which might have put down any fish, and the cattle upstream were wallowing and turning loose a lot of silt. In short I was skunked. I saw no sign of a trout.

The stream appears to have tremendous potential, however. Some old stream restoration work needs to be maintained—that might help. And reducing the silt generated by the cattle will help even more. If the Susquehannock Fly Fishers (whoever they are) lease the water, there must be fish there, but I never found them.

Gingrich Run—3

Tiny to nonexistent.

Hammer Creek—4

This nice stream rises in the limestone springs that produce water for Michter's Distillery, a neat old outfit dating back to the eighteenth century but still running off Pennsylvania whiskey. The stream is maybe 12 to 18 feet wide and has some elodea and other vegetation. The water is cool, but there is a plentiful supply of silt in the stream. Overall this is no world-class limestoner. No trout were in evidence, though the stream is stocked, but there were a few chubs.

Killinger Creek—5

This lovely small limestoner appears to be exactly what a limestone stream should be: in a beautiful setting, cold, lots of overhanging grasses and cress beds, and good amounts of aquatic weed. The part I was on is maybe 6 to 10 feet wide and is a fine meadow stream. It's not to be confused with the special-regulation area of the Little Lehigh as far as fish population is concerned; however, I did take one fine holdover brown of about 14 inches on a hopper, and my clumsy wading terrified another. On the whole, it appears prettier than it is productive, but it has potential. The fish most likely come up from the Quittapahilla.

Mill Creek—6

This pastoral stream flows through lovely farm country, which, however, causes its thermal problems in midsummer. There are some substantial limestone springs where the fish congregate during warm weather. The stocked stream is about 20 to 30 feet wide and has some pretty water, both meadow stretches and some fairly active pocket water which flows over limestone outcrops. The only fish I turned up were stockers; but it is a pleasant stream to spend some time on, at least early in the year.

Quittapahilla Creek—7

This is a substantial stream, around 50 to 60 feet wide just above the Millard quarry where I fished it. It runs cold and has a nice solid bottom, some riffles, and large, deep pools. It is a stocked stream, but frankly it seems to be suited more for smallmouths than trout, and it has an ample supply of carp. The stream is nice water and should harbor a substantial population of trout as well as all those carp; however, none were in a sipping mood, and my nymphing was not deep enough for the relatively strong currents in this sizable stream. I did catch a glimpse of what I am certain was a trout sucking in minutiae under some brush. I did my best minutia presentation, got a take, and promptly missed the fish, so I really can't say what it was. Nice stream, but not memorable.

There is more to this stream, though. According to Don Douple this is a classic example of a stream coming back to health. Formerly it was heavily polluted, but construction of a new sewer plant removed much of the problem. While I am outspoken on the problems that often accompany sewer plants on trout streams, I will give credit where it is due: this is a case where the installation of a sewer plant resulted in a stream's being cleaned up enough to be a trout fishery again.

Snitz Creek—8

With 82-degree water and banks that were trampled flat, I felt there was somewhere else that needed my urgent attention.

Tulpehocken Creek—9

The "Tully" is much loved in the Reading area for its fine water below Blue Marsh Dam and the special-regulation water there. Here in Lebanon County above Myerstown it is a much smaller, more intimate limestone spring creek. It runs about 20 to 30 feet wide and has clear, cold water. It has suffered some indignities from the cattle ranging its banks, but still it appears to be what a limestone trout stream should be. The stream is stocked and I feel pretty confident there are fish there. But I couldn't buy one. At the upper section of the stretch I fished, there apparently is a fish hatchery, and this often drives out wild fish below. It is fine-looking water, although in one place I nearly fell into what appeared to be an underwater sinkhole.

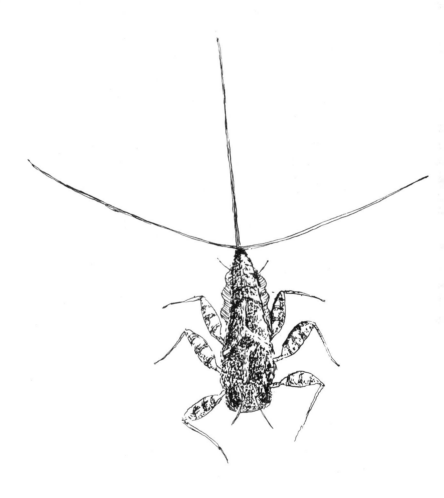

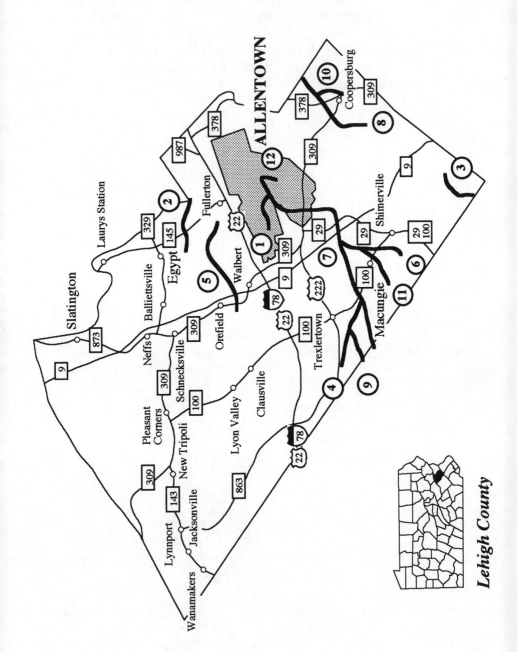

Lehigh County

LEHIGH COUNTY

This large, populous county may not be the obvious place to go looking for fine wild trout fishing on limestone streams, and it definitely is not a place to seek out a wilderness experience. But if you don't mind having company, this is an area of really great trout waters.

The Little Lehigh is clearly at the top of the list. It's a large and varied stream, urban or pastoral, full of silt or gravel, with wild trout in some areas and shoulder-to-shoulder stockers in others. Its feeders—Cedar Creek, Trout Creek, and Iron Run—have all the characteristics of limestone waters. They are all urbanized to greater or lesser extents. Trout Creek is about the most urbanized stream I have ever caught a wild trout in, flowing as it does through downtown Allentown. But the water quality is good as the wild trout will attest.

Civic leaders in the area had the foresight to establish greenbelt parks along the stream corridors, so while you might be fishing in built-up areas, it appears that the stream corridors will not be built up any further. The fishing here is really good, and these streams have held their own in spite of heavy urban development. Many people travel considerable distances to fish the Little Lehigh and it is worth the trip, but it would be a more satisfying experience if more of the stream and its feeders would get some of that attention. Beyond the Little Lehigh system there are some other pleasant streams, even if they aren't up to the high standards of the Little Lehigh.

Cedar Creek—1

What's in a name? Besides the many Spring Creeks in Pennsylvania, which include some phenomenal fisheries, a stream named Cedar Creek or Cedar Run is likely to offer good fishing—and this one is no exception. This fine limestone run is a feeder to the much more famous Little Lehigh. Much of the stream flows through municipal parks, and while the banks may be a bit too zealously mowed, it does not appear to have disturbed the fine population of wild browns. The stream is medium sized, perhaps 20 feet or so wide, with relatively few large holes or bends. It doesn't seem to have much great holding water, but the fish are there. They have been handled a time or two, however, so they aren't easy. If stalking selectively feeding wild browns is your game, and you don't insist on a wilderness setting, this stream is a winner. The trike hatch is a good time to do a population survey, as all the small to medium-sized fish are on the surface.

Cedar Run in Tioga County is one of the classic freestone streams in the Commonwealth, while a like-named stream in Clinton County is a lovely and prolific limestoner. Even the numerous Spring creeks in the state do not compare to these three fine streams.

Coplay Creek—2

This is a small, stocked limestone stream, maybe 15 to 20 feet wide, with good holding water and some very large holes. While all I caught were stockers—but good numbers of them—I did see what appeared to be a different year class with much smaller trout, which presumably would be wild. I couldn't get hold of any to verify. The water is cold and must hold fish well through the summer. There has been extensive channel relocation, and you'll find more quarry spoil piles than pastoral meadows, but here again, the stream is up against some stiff competition and just doesn't measure up to some of the excellent fisheries nearby. Nevertheless, I do think that it is worth learning more about.

Hosensack Creek—3

This substantial stream flows just a short distance between the major feeders where it begins and its discharge point at the Perkiomen above Green Lane Reservoir. It has some wide spots—up to about 50 feet—but generally it is 25 feet or so wide and runs cool to cold. In many ways it resembles Cooks Creek in nearby Bucks County in that it flows over red sandstone and looks like a freestone stream but receives substantial and frequent inputs of cold spring water from limestone springs resulting in stream temperatures of 58 degrees. Also like Cooks Creek, it has wild browns and a few stocked rainbows and brookies that might have wandered up from the Perkiomen. It did not look overly fertile, but sulphurs and a few caddis were in evidence in mid-June. "No Trespassing" signs abound, so take care.

Iron Run—4

This small limestoner is a major feeder to the Little Lehigh. It runs about 20 feet wide and has some stretches of model spring creek water. There are wild browns as well as some stockers that have swum up to get to its cold summer water (about 60 degrees). There also are carp, which, until recognized for what they were, nearly caused me to have cardiac arrest one afternoon. A combination of poor agricultural practices and increasing urbanization has caused some substantial siltation problems. But it is a splendid small limestoner, worth a side trip.

Jordan Creek—5

This heavily stocked stream is mainly a place to disperse opening-day pressure. By early June it was barely flowing, although there were a few large, deep holes with water in them. Avoid this one unless early-season hatchery products are your idea of trout fishing.

A year after writing this description, I got word that the current state-record rainbow had been taken from Jordan Creek. This hapless behemoth probably spent two, maybe three, days miserable and disoriented in the stream before being derricked out by the lucky angler. So perhaps a slight revision is in order: this one can be safely avoided unless early-season, occasionally very large, hatchery products are your idea of trout fishing.

Leibert Creek—6

I was on this stream near Macungie. It should be a small stream, and, considering its flow, I guess it is. However, it has been severely degraded by poor storm-water management, so it is now about five streams wide and one-fifth of a stream deep. No holding water, no nuthin'. It is a write-off.

Little Lehigh Creek—7

No doubt the Little Lehigh is one of the most important limestone streams in the state and, for that matter, the nation. It is a substantial stream, up to 50 feet wide in the section of interest to trout fishermen. With substantial limestone springs along its length, it runs cool all year long.

Considerable stretches of the stream banks are in parkland systems, so access is not a problem. This is not a small point. The parklands assure that the banks are mowed to the edge of the stream—a mixed blessing—but the park folks have done a good job of controlling bank erosion. The open, mowed meadows adjacent to the stream are great places for children to play.

The stream has many personalities. The catch-and-release stretch has all the characteristics of a freestone stream: pools and riffles, large boulders, flow over ledges of bedrock, but with numerous springs to keep the water cold and fertile. It also gets a lot of fishing pressure over a substantial population of fish, both wild and stocked. And there are some monsters here. Some time back, Don Douple caught a 27-inch 9-pounder on this stretch.

It is a pity that so few people venture outside the catch-and-release area. Locals feel that the best fishing on the stream is on the "open" water, which gets little pressure after early season. A good trike hatch makes the open water particularly attractive. Outside the catch-and-release stretch the stream begins to show its true diversity. There are sections of flat, weedy, limestone spring-run water, as well as stretches of deep pools and fast water. There are areas of the stream where virtually all the fish are wild, both the predominant browns and some brookies. Small nymphs are preferred by many locals, as are terrestrials, especially ants, probably the most underrated fly there is.

"Seek and ye shall find" is the motto for this stream. It is a large stream system, with all sorts of fascinating variety. While special-regulation fishing is good for the ego, most of the stream has a lovely mix of conditions, with little pressure and wild trout in good numbers. There is an ongoing siltation problem that needs attention, and increasing urbanization is depleting some springs, but in spite of the problems this prolific stream is far and away the best urban stream around.

The Little Lehigh Chapter of TU has worked out a hatch calendar. Joe Kohler indicates the listing is pretty true for area streams as well as the Little Lehigh. He also has given us two last-minute additions: the mid-June emergence of the yellow drake *(Ephemera varia)* and the mid-August evening appearance of the Huge Slate Drake *(Hexagenia atrocaudata)*.

LITTLE LEHIGH EMERGENCE CHART

KEY

_____ Major Hatch

- - - - - - - - - - Sporadic

	Mar.	Apr.	May	June	July	Aug.	Sept.	Oct.
Midges (Diptera)	──	─ - -	- - - -	- - ──	- -	──	──	──
Blue Quill (*Baetis vagen*)	──	─ -	- - - ──		- ─	- - ─		
Iron Blue Dun (*Paraleptophlebia mollis*)		──						
Spotted Sedge (*Hydropsyche alternans*)		────						
Orange Crane Fly (*Tipula*)		──						
Olive Sedge (*Rhyacophila bosalis*)			─ - -					
Minute Blue-winged Olive (*Baetis levitans*)			──	─ - - -				
Pale Evening Dun (*Ephemerella dorothea*)			────					
Little Sulphur Dun (*Epeorus vitreus*)				── - - -				
Light Cahill (*Stenacron canadense*)				────				
Little Yellow Dun (*Leucrocuta hebe*)			- - -	- - -	- - -	- - -	- -	
White-winged Black Quill (*Tricorythodes stygiatus*)				────	──	──	──	──
Little Evening Sulphur (*Heptagenia minerva*)					- - -	- - -	- - -	
Black Caddis (*Dolophilodes nigrita*)					── -	- - -	- - -	- -

Saucon Creek—8

This varied, stocked stream used to be a favorite of Charlie Fox when he attended college nearby. Regrettably, it has fallen on hard times, although it appears to be fighting its way back and it could return to its former greatness. It is not a long stream, but it develops into a sizable body of water in a relatively short length, perhaps 50 to 70 feet wide in the lower sections near Hellertown.

The water runs cool during hot, humid times. It resembles the nearby Bushkill in many respects, although at this time it is definitely an inferior fishery.

Dr. John Hampsey of the Monocacy Chapter of TU advises that since New Jersey Zinc ceased its mining operation in the Saucon Valley a number of years ago, this stream has slowly but steadily improved, and it has the potential of becoming once again the best limestoner in the area. Considering what else is around, that is strong talk!

There are some wild fish in the uppermost water, with some fine wild browns turning up in places. The lower water also might have some wild fish, but I was unable to verify. The small fish I did turn up were most likely wild, but all were pretty serious about achieving long releases. One brown in particular, about 7 inches, pounced on my nymph and, upon feeling the hook, promptly disgorged a 2-inch minnow and set about the business of achieving freedom, which didn't take very long. I saw a number of other, larger fish, but they were too tough for me. Apparently the sulphur hatch is prime time here, as it is on most limestoners. There were a good number of fly fishers for late June. Nice stream. Tough fish!

Schaefer Run—9

This tiny rivulet is too small to be of much interest to trout fishermen. It eventually joins and contributes to the flow of the Little Lehigh, but in its own right it is just too small to amount to much.

South Branch Saucon Creek—10

It's a lovely stream, maybe 20 to 40 feet wide, with lots of nice holding water, nice clean gravel, and lots of insects (including ferocious mosquitoes). I couldn't buy a trout, however, which surprised me because the stream is stocked. No evidence of any trout at all, although there were lots of chubs.

Swabia Creek—11

This small stream (mostly less than 10 feet wide) is one of the many feeders to the Little Lehigh—but not one of the memorable ones. On the other hand, it is better than one description I have heard: a ditch in a cornfield. It is small and quite brushy, but it has decent holding water and runs cool all summer. I was unable to turn up any wild trout or precious few stockers (it is a stocked stream). However, my hunch is that it's a better stream than I am a fisherman, so I can't complain too loudly. There are trout there through the summer, and its cool waters must help the Little Lehigh. But in this region of amazing trout fisheries, this stream is a fourth stringer. There are just too many better streams nearby.

Trout Creek—12

This amazing feeder to the Little Lehigh is a TU project waiting to happen. The lowest stretch, about half a mile long just above the confluence with the Little Lehigh, flows through downtown Allentown. I saw an abandoned trash incinerator, pipes sticking out of cinder banks dripping evil-looking fluids, and all kinds of plastic trash. There are endless culverts and bridges, all leading to a large, illegal dumping area. The stream is decent sized— maybe 20 feet or so wide—and, incredibly, holds fine wild browns, as a limestone stream should. What an amazing demonstration of the powers of limestone streams.

Farther up, the stream flows through one of those pleasant Allentown stream corridor Greenway parks. In this case the banks are less manicured than those of the Little Lehigh and Cedar creeks. With 56-degree water in late July and the dependable trikes pirouetting above every late-summer morning, the stream has a lot to recommend it. Apparently some form of renewal project is slated for the evil-looking (and smelling) lowest part of the watershed. Most of the lower watershed is on public land and cleaning it up will not be easy, but what an asset a clean Trout Creek would be to Allentown!

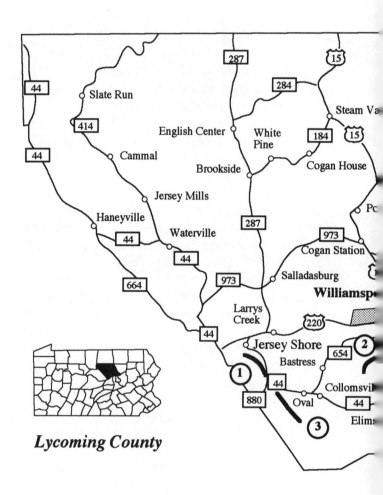

Lycoming County

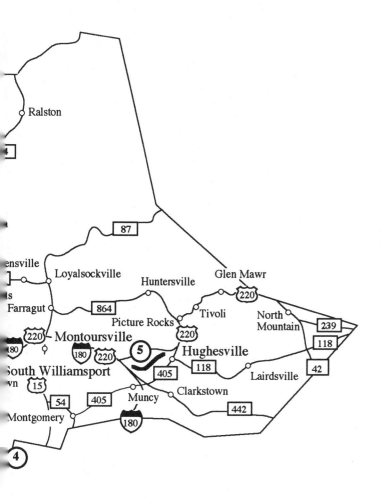

LYCOMING COUNTY

This area is well known to most Pennsylvania outdoorsmen. It is the big woods of north-central Pennsylvania, land full of deer and bear and some of the state's finest trout streams.

Pine Creek and the Loyalsock, Cedar, and Slate runs are justly famous freestone waters that rank at or near the top in any listing of trout streams in the Commonwealth. These are the streams that come to mind when knowledgeable fishermen think about Lycoming County.

There is more to Lycoming County, though, than freestone waters. Antes Creek is typical limestone water, surrounded by classic freestone streams for a good way in all directions. Mosquito Creek has large numbers of trout, some wild, and, in spite of its freestone appearance, gets a good dose of limestone water to keep it cold and running strong through the summer.

No question, going up into Lycoming County is a delightful way to experience the outdoors. While the freestone streams will always be the most famous, those limestone streams are fine fisheries.

Antes Creek—1

This is an important stream, with only one problem: there is a fellow who leases most of it, and he has put a sign on every tree along his section. It is a beautiful limestone stream, of good size, typically 30 to 40 feet wide. It appears to rise right out of the ground as a full-fledged stream with frigid, mineral-laden water. There is a fairly steep gradient and great holding water. But for most of its length, signs clearly indicate that whatever you want to do, do it elsewhere. Ernie Schwiebert told me that above the posted water is a section where the fishing is positively heavenly but is controlled and even more heavily posted by someone else.

I didn't have an invitation for either section, but I did find a short section downstream that wasn't posted, had a good population of wild browns, and had 60-degree water in August. One particularly inviting run just pleaded for a stonefly nymph to drift through it. I tried, and sure enough the line suddenly quit drifting along with the current and I was fast into something impressive. The fish ran me downstream through several holes, but I eventually corralled a magnificent 17-inch brown, which I had lassoed when my nymph formed a noose that somehow had tightened around the fish's "wrist." Other fish were a good deal smaller, but they were fine wild fish, the way trout should look.

There is a huge, round hole, just below the railroad overpass and those ubiquitous signs, that is just about the largest pool I have ever seen on a Pennsylvania trout stream. It is almost perfectly round, as if a meteorite hit there, and it appears bottomless. I'll bet there's a fish in it as long as my leg.

Mosquito Creek—2

This is a nice stream, maybe 15 to 30 feet wide. It looks for all the world like a freestone stream, but it runs cool enough (69-degree water in August) to hint at upstream limestone springs. However, it's in an area plastered with "Stay the Hell Out" signs. Cottage owners in some sections have felt the need to dam up the stream to "improve" it. And they might have brought in some buckets of trout, as well, because I caught both wild and stocker brookies (all legal sizes only) and browns. Fishing here is not a wilderness experience, and besides, the cottage owners probably would take a dim view of outsiders lifting their fish from the stream.

Nippenose Creek—3

This "stream" is a dry bed.

Spring Creek—4

This is a pleasant, small (maybe 20 feet wide or so) stream that gets stocked by the Fish Commission. By mid-July, when I was there, very few were left. I did terrify one, but saw no substantial trout population. You have to see the crawfish population to believe it. The bottom is clean gravel, and the temperatures are on the warm side, but I think some reproduction might be possible. All in all it appears to be a freestone stream, and not a memorable one.

Unnamed Stream near Muncy—5

Although there is a quarry nearby to attest to the limestone in the ground, this stream shows minimal limestone influence and is just another small, upstate "crick" like countless others. It's not a mandatory stop on the limestoner circuit.

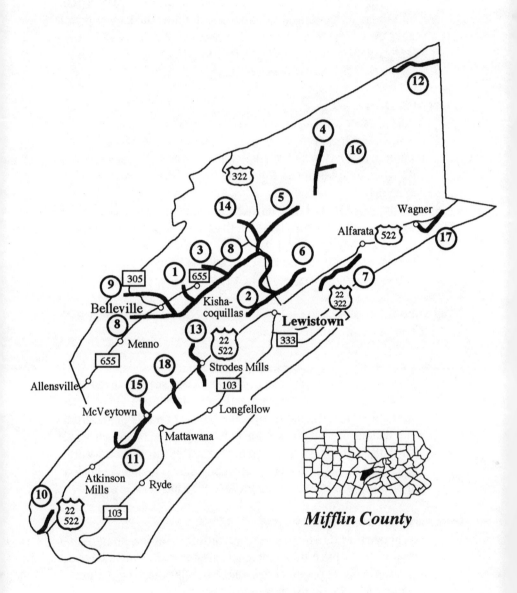

Mifflin County

MIFFLIN COUNTY

This area has done a great job of keeping its treasures hidden. Mifflin County's limestone trout waters should rank high (well, maybe not as high as Centre County's, but that's unfair competition).

A significant stretch of the nicest water on Penns Creek is in the county, as are the surprising Honey Creek, the lovely little Tea Creek, the heavily posted Coffee Creek, the fine little Alexander Spring Run, the astonishingly prolific Long Hollow Run, and the three little streams at McVeytown: Musser, Town, and Wakefield runs.

Everybody knows that for limestone fishing you go to Cumberland County. A few, more knowledgeable people know that Centre County has really great fishing due to deep deposits of carbonates, and a few realize that in Lehigh and Northampton counties there are some neat streams. But no one seems to be aware of Mifflin County's waters.

Alexander Spring Run—1

This tiny spring run is ideal limestone water. It is generally less than 10 feet wide, but it has a number of deep holding pockets, especially around road crossings. It has plenty of aquatic vegetation, overhanging meadow growth, and 56-degree water in mid-August. It also has an absolutely beautiful abandoned log-and-stone house, which I hope someone picks up and brings back to life. This gorgeous little stream has some lovely wild browns in it. The best one I caught was maybe 11 inches, but probably there are much bigger ones there. One road crossing with a very low bridge has "all the trout in the world" under it. I failed repeatedly to get a decent cast under there from a discreet enough distance that I wouldn't spook the fish. I was so intent on catching a few that I didn't notice a large bovine approaching. I saw quickly that it was a male of the species, and I was in his meadow, but only for a few seconds. Those trout are still there, gently sipping tidbits off the surface. This is a neat little stream, if you like small-stream angling, as I do. There is considerably more to this stream than that meadow, and the fish seem to be liberally scattered. This is the sort of stream to keep in mind during heavy rains. Unlike the larger streams in the area, this one would not get badly out of shape.

Buck Run—2

This small stream is 6 to 12 feet wide, with 80-degree water. It had a wide, shallow streambed when I was there, and it's quite possible that it might dry up. Not trout water.

Coffee Creek—3

It seems that someone around Reedsville went wild with grocery names for the local streams. There's Honey Creek, Tea Creek, and Coffee Creek, a small limestoner, maybe 10 to 15 feet wide, most of it leased and stocked water. Some impoundments, as well as the presence of cattle, have not helped the stream. Nevertheless, it is lovely, with watercress beds and fine, fat browns. A friend caught a 13-inch brown that still had parr marks on it. At the upper end the stream comes out of a cave below the knoll where an Amish family lives. The stream is short, maybe a mile at most, with most of this section leased. A polite request got me in, but I suspect this would not be the general case. The only fish I could fool was a lovely fat brown with beautiful coloration. My host said it was a stocker. If so, it was far and away the nicest stocked trout I have ever seen, with full pectorals and bright red spots against a butter yellow flank. This is a lovely little stream, but there are others as good in the area that aren't private waters, so there is no need to intrude.

Havice Creek—4

This small, stocked stream (about 15 feet wide) has some limestone influence, just about all of it bad. It is basically a freestone stream that runs through meadows where cattle pummel it. When it enters the limestone area, it promptly disappears underground, presumably forming part of the major spring that establishes Honey Creek. Some stream restoration work narrowed and deepened this water, which is all to the good, but it would be hard to call this a limestone creek.

Honey Creek—5

This substantial stream is sort of a junior grade Penns Creek. It looks like Penns Creek, it is somewhat smaller (but then so is just about any trout stream in the state), and it runs colder, with 61-degree water in August. Honey Creek is around 50 or 60 feet wide in general and rises from a major spring that is surrounded by barbed wire, uninviting signs, and, for all I know, land mines. I got the distinct impression my presence was not wanted. The stream has nice pools, riffles, and runs, with nice brown trout in its off-color waters. I never have done all that well on the stream, but I have seen others do extremely well, so I don't blame the stream. A friend lost a bragging-sized fish there after a morning of turkey hunting nearby, and the Fish Commission's electrofishing results indicate a substantial wild brown trout population. The fish are there, and if you are good enough, you will fool some. I only managed to fool a few juveniles and a large blind one. There is some water that is closed on Sundays, and this can be a nasty surprise if you had planned on a weekend of fishing. Otherwise, this is a lovely stream and worth a visit.

Hungry Run—6

This stream looks pleasant enough, about 20 feet or so wide, with reasonably cool water in midsummer. No trout turned up the first time I visited, but the water was up a bit and discolored, so I worked in a repeat trip and got the same results in good water conditions. There should be trout here, but if so, they are very clever or very scarce.

Jacks Creek—7

This substantial stream really is smallmouth/muskie water. At 50 to 60 feet wide and 80 degrees, it has none of the earmarks of trout water. Down below Maitland there are some limestone springs that lower the water temperature to 75 degrees, but I couldn't find any evidence of trout. Maybe there are some, but they weren't hanging out at the spring's mouth, which surprised me. This is very marginal habitat for trout in midsummer.

Kishacoquillas Creek—8

This is a very substantial stream below Reedsville, where it's about 100 feet wide, and it is intimidating to wade in the heavy water of the narrows above Yeagertown. However, it is worth taking up the challenge.

With the cold water of Tea Creek, and more particularly Honey Creek, this is a nice stretch of water with temperatures in the upper 60s in mid-August. There's a good head of trout, mostly wild fish though the water is stocked, and they know their bugs.

Above the infusion of that cold water things mellow out a bit: the temperature is higher and the trout population decidedly leaner. Smaller amounts of cold limestone water enter from Coffee Creek and Alexander Spring Run. In general the upper stream suffers thermal problems in midsummer, while the lower water maintains a good head of fish.

In addition to what appeared to be a profuse Ausable Wulff hatch, stoneflies are abundant in the heavy pocket sections of the lower water. Most other flies will appear in their appropriate time slots, as well.

This is a very nice, substantial stream, and it can handle a lot of fishermen. For years as I hurried to meccas in Centre County, I wondered about this stream, but that was before I learned how good the limestone streams of Mifflin County are!

Little Kishacoquillas Creek—9

This stream appears to be a freestoner at Belleville, where it joins its larger namesake. There is no evidence of trout or good habitat for them.

Long Hollow Run—10

This small stream is only about 10 feet wide at its widest point, but it is a veritable fish heaven. There is a large limestone spring about a half mile above the confluence with the Juniata, and the fish are literally crammed into this section. I saw wild browns in at least four year classes—probably more, as one was well over 20 inches. This stream, with its challenge of too many trout, was a bear to fish! I would ease up to the bottom of a riffle and look at the pool above until I located the trout holding in the shallows of the pool's tail. Then I would make a very gentle cast to it, at which point five or six other trout that I hadn't seen would panic and shoot into the middle of the pool, where they would mill around with maybe twenty or so others, all totally spooked. I caught only one fish, a heavy 13-inch brown that was perfect in every respect. The rest I panicked with appalling regularity.

Above the major limestone spring there are still a few fish, but nothing like the concentration below. I went until I hit a series of "Posted" signs. There may be more good water farther above, but down where I was the section wasn't aesthetically appealing—fast-food joints on a high bank on one side and on the other

side shacks with upside-down Studebakers on the lawns. The fish
didn't seem to mind, though.

Musser Run—11

This is the least impressive of the three limestone streams in the
immediate vicinity of McVeytown. The stream is 10 to 15 feet wide
and runs through meadows where it gets pretty heavy cattle traffic. It is a stocked stream, and the water temperatures in midsummer are pretty agreeable. But I saw no trout when I was there.

Penns Creek (See Centre County, Penns Creek, page 88.)—12

Strodes Run—13

This stream is more or less a twin of nearby Wakefield Run, but it
is a bit larger, about 15 to 20 feet wide, and has identical 68-degree
water. It is largely freestone but has clear-cut limestone influence.
It is also stocked and has a decent population of wild browns. I
didn't raise anything large, but I think there are better parts than
where I was. A very pleasant area, with nice little streams.

Tea Creek—14

Some places are blessed, and certainly the tiny hamlet of
Reedsville is one of these: Honey, Tea, and Kishacoquillas creeks
all join together in the town. Although the smallest of the three,
with an average width of 15 to 20 feet, Tea Creek may be the best.
It runs frigid all summer long (56-degree water in early August). It
rises as a full-blown creek from a large spring located exactly under Route 322. (I wonder how many fans hurrying to see Penn
State realize that they are driving right on top of the spring head
of a lovely trout stream!) While not a major stream, it is prolific.
As there is a very steep gradient—in places the stream seems to
be vertical—forget any thoughts of silky currents. What you'll find
is pocket water, a rare thing on limestone streams, and pocket water means fish that aren't hassled! The fish are perfect, bright,
wild browns, and some are substantially larger than the 14-inch-
er that took my stonefly nymph in heavy water. Locals talk of large
fish extracted by skillful bait fishermen.

About the only bad news is the millpond in town, which
warms the water and curtails Tea Creek's plunge down to its

confluence with the two larger streams. This stream is a little gem—everything a trout stream should be. While it has heavy water, there are also a few flats reminiscent of spring runs. The fish are there. I can't imagine why this lovely stream isn't better known.

Town Run—15

This nice little stream flows through the village of McVeytown. Sometimes it is only 5 feet wide or less and at other times it opens up to 15 feet. It is a high-gradient stream, with good pocket water, some waterfalls over prominent ledges, and 67-degree water. It is stocked but evidently has some wild fish. The only trout I got my hands on was a heavy 15-inch brown, which appeared to have never been inside a hatchery. The stream seems to get very heavy pressure, but some fish must make it through.

Treaster Run—16

The lowest stretch of this nice-sized—20 to 25 feet wide—stream runs over limestone before its confluence with Havice Creek. (Actually, Havice Creek is a dry streambed at this point, but my maps show it as the surviving stream.) I didn't see much limestone influence, but I did find a very nice stream. It apparently isn't stocked in the lower area, although it is farther up. There are, however, good numbers of wild browns; I turned up six in a short time on a bright afternoon. The best one I got was about 13 inches, but there are undoubtedly larger ones there. I noticed lots of overhanging alders and other brush, which make the stream seem much smaller than it really is. The water is very clear, the bottom is clean gravel, and the fish are spooky and tough to reach because of all that vegetation.

A short distance below the stretch I fished there is a substantial cave, reputedly with large logs stuck well up inside it. During periods of heavy rainfall, the cave spews out large flows of water and detritus. In addition to the fine trout, I scared out a woodcock and turned up two world-class morels, those equally delectable and safe wild mushrooms. I kept the morels and released the trout. The stream seems to be a wonderful example of Murphy's Law adapted for small-stream fishermen: the best water will always have a fence or a downed tree across it. In spite of the many frustrations, this is a stream worth fishing.

Wagner Run—17

This is a tiny, unnamed stream, but Wagner is the nearest town. It really is a dry streambed.

Wakefield Run—18

This is the third of the streams in the McVeytown area. It is 10 to 15 feet wide and flows through meadows where cattle wreak havoc. However, the water temperature remains very positive at 68 degrees, and there is a decent population of wild browns. I didn't move anything very large, but then I didn't see any great holding water, although I think there probably are better areas. Overall, it was a pleasure to poke around in this area.

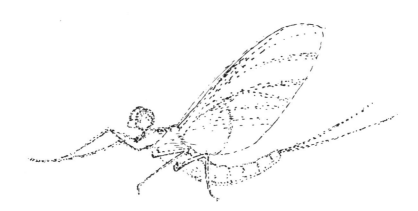

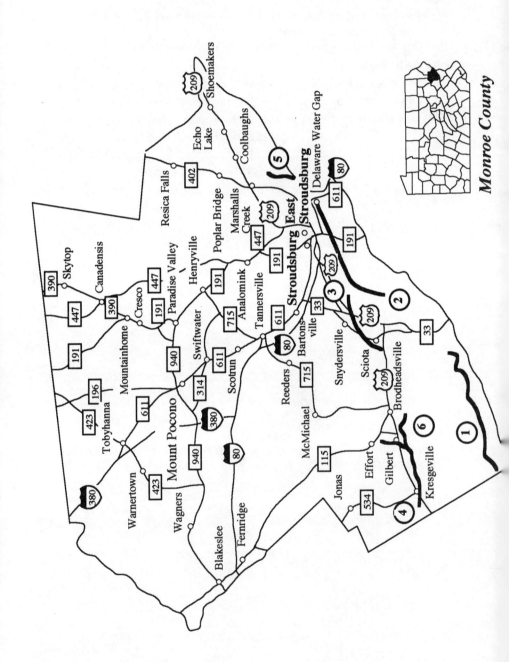

Monroe County

MONROE COUNTY

This represents the last vestiges of a limestone area as one travels north into the Poconos. While basically a freestone area, there are some limestone influences on a few streams here.

A very narrow band of limestone runs along the southern edge of the county and gives some water to two streams there: Cherry Creek and Aquashicola Creek. Neither of these streams would be considered major additions to any list of limestone streams, but it is fair to say they show some limestone influence, and both are decent, honest streams.

Aquashicola Creek—1

This small stream has some problems, but it also has some good things going for it. Above Chicola Lake, where I fished it, the stream is about 15 feet wide. The bottom is clean gravel without a lot of deep pools. But that's not bad. It looks like a freestone stream, but the cold water might come from a limestone seam that parallels the stream. The water was stocked and a healthy 67 degrees on a hot day.

There were loads of wild brookies the day I was there, and they seemed very content, which is fine for the brookies, but frustrating for the fisherman. I did eventually take one.

The main problem might not be a problem at all: streamside vegetation arches over the stream from each side and meets and tangles in the middle. The effect is to make this stream as close to unfishable as any I've seen. Don Douple refers to this growth as a brush tunnel. There are a number of places deeper than wide, but they are basically unfishable because of the vegetation. Even Paul Nale, who can fish in a teacup, admitted that much of it is too brushy for his brand of spin fishing. There are a few stretches that don't sport "No Trespassing" signs, and for the masochist they offer brookies in the upper water and browns lower down. This is a tough stream to fish!

Don Baylor confirms that there are some limestone springs feeding the stream giving it higher alkalinity than most streams in the area. Nevertheless, it is basically a freestoner. He indicated there is a good trike hatch as well as *Ephemerella lata* and substantial Morning Olives (size 16) in late June, as well as *Ephemera varia* in mid-June and *Hexagenia* later in the summer.

Downstream the evident geology is red siltstone beds, with warmer water and all the "No Trespassing" signs in the world. Not inviting, even though there are trout.

Cherry Creek—2

This stream is about 25 to 30 feet wide at Route 191 and has good holding water of 75 degrees. It also has loads of overhanging brush, and I do mean loads. I turned up plenty of chubs, but no trout. There is some vegetation in the stream, but the general feel of this place is freestone. There are cooler spots indicating substantial springs, and there is even some evidence of stream restoration in parts. This is a nice stream, and while I didn't turn up any trout, I expect there are some there.

Don Baylor, who lives in the area and who wrote a neat little booklet called "Hatches of the Poconos," knows this stream and was able to confirm that it is a limestoner, with much higher alkalinity and pH than neighboring streams. The insect life is also unique in the area, Don says. In some sections there is a tremendous trike hatch. He also mentions Blue-winged Olives *(Baetis)* of about size 20, and an impressive *Potamanthus* (large, light-colored mayfly) hatch in June. Further, there is *Ephemera varia*, the substantial mayfly that shows up in considerable numbers in mid- to late June.

He also confirms my suspicions that there are wild browns in fishable numbers. The down side is that there is a great deal of posted land, much of it aimed at hunters, but the signs are there and must be respected.

McMichael Creek—3

The lower section of this stocked stream is wide—up to 60 feet—and shallow. It looks like classic freestone water, but I saw no sign of trout. (I fished a short way above a golf course outside Stroudsburg during an extended heat wave, so the fish might have moved to more suitable surroundings.) Up near Kellersville the stream is smaller, maybe 30 to 40 feet wide, and passes between two limestone quarries. Although limestone influence seems marginal, it is a nice stretch of water, with fine holding spots, productive-looking riffles, and 63-degree water in late June. There is a good head of wild browns, including some nice-sized ones. I didn't see much insect activity, but the fine, plump fish prove there must be good aquatic life.

Pohopoco Creek—4

The geologic maps indicate that the area between Kresgeville and Gilbert has no limestone, at least at the surface, yet this stream shows many characteristics of a limestoner, including a lot of the right aquatic vegetation and attractive water temperatures. This is not a tiny mountain brook, being at least 30 to 50 feet wide near Kresgeville. It's a good deal smaller at Gilbert, which isn't far upstream, indicating something remarkable happens in a relatively short distance. There are all the outward signs of a limestone stream, but it just doesn't match the geology.

Don Baylor, who keeps track of water quality and insect life on all streams in the area, confirms that some limestone water flows into this basically freestone stream, and in Monroe County this limestone is a blessing, because acid rain is a real problem. The stream is stocked.

The main hatches are *Hydropsyche* (size 14 to 16 dun-colored caddis) intermittent mid-May through September, sulphurs and Blue-winged Olives in mid-June, *Isonychia* early and late in the season, and a good *Tricorythodes* hatch in the summer.

Shawnee Creek—5

This tiny stream has virtually nothing going for it. It is at most 5 feet wide and has warm water and no noticeable limestone influence. To add insult to injury, it is the most heavily posted stream I have seen. I don't think I missed anything by not sneaking in.

Weir Creek—6

Like nearby Pohopoco Creek, this stream is an enigma: it has evident limestone characteristics (it is a limestone spring run from all visible signs) in an area where my geologic maps indicate no surface limestone. However, there might be limestone a short distance below the surface. Whatever the situation, this small stream, maybe 10 to 20 feet wide, is for all the world a limestone spring run, with seductive currents, lots of watercress and other alkaline-loving vegetation, and tough sipping fish. I say tough, because I was unable to convince any of them to take any of my presentations. Much of the stream flows through apparently bottomless bogs, which makes the going exceptionally difficult, even scary. In addition, the "banks" have the consistency of slightly lumpy jelly, so my movements managed to create waves that put fish down just about three feet farther than I could cast. The bottom looked solid enough to wade, but the water was generally deeper than my hippers. The long and short of it: I came, I saw, and I was thoroughly conquered. I did see a number of what appeared to be trout fleeing wildly in various directions. I saw one heart-stopping brute take off downstream looking like a nuclear submarine. All of them were totally unimpressed by my clumsy offerings. Interesting stream, but it was better than I was.

Paul Nale, who lives in the area, says the stream holds wild brookies and browns. He also claims limestone is there, no matter what my geologic maps say.

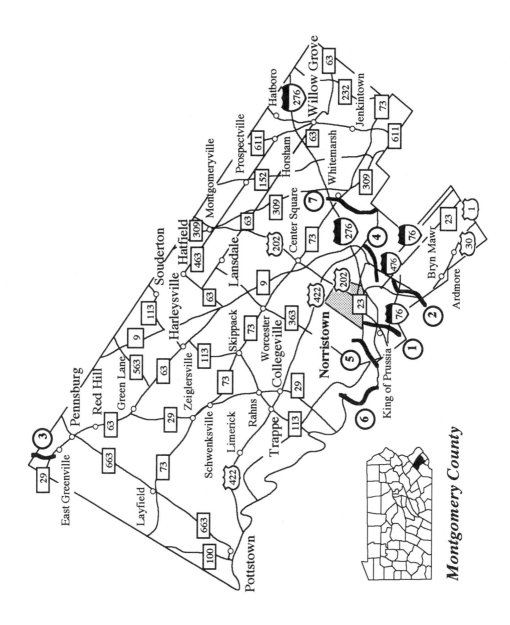

Montgomery County

MONTGOMERY COUNTY

There are a few limestone belts running through southern Montgomery County, and they influence to some extent at least one stream: Trout Run. Also, Valley Creek—a true limestoner—flows for a mile or so (below the limestone belt but with limestone water quality) before it meets the Schuylkill at Washington's Headquarters in Valley Forge Park.

The heavy urbanization of southern Montgomery County has blown out the streams. Gulph and Wissahickon creeks, and Abrams and Trout runs all have problems that are the result of overuse of the limited water resources.

Trout Run has a few sections that probably can support trout, but there are problems at each end of such stretches—the whole stream disappears underground, or there are massive, poorly controlled discharges of sewer effluent. This is basically a dead stream.

Perhaps I'm being crabby to complain that "only" Valley Creek represents a true limestone fishery in this urbanized area, but it is a darn shame that the other waters have been lost to poorly planned development.

Abrams Run—1

This small stream is thoroughly urbanized and essentially bombed out. It is maybe 10 feet wide and has what could be some decent holding water. I saw long strands of filamentous algae, 80-degree water, some shopping carts, and a few suckers.

Gulph Creek—2

This poor stream is thoroughly bombed out. It is maybe 10 to 15 feet wide and appears to be freestone. The water isn't really warm, but it isn't really cool either. At 76 degrees some trout could hang on, but there were no signs of any when I was there.

Hosensack Creek (See Lehigh County, Hosensack Creek, page 176.)—3

Plymouth Creek—4

This dry creekbed is basically a harsh environment.

Trout Run—5

This stream parallels Abrams Run. The two are pretty close together and both have major problems. This one is about 15 to 20 feet wide below King of Prussia. It has good cold water and looks like it could very easily support trout. Upstream there are all sorts of problems related to massive urbanization—large parking lots dumping storm water directly into the stream and a massive noxious discharge from a sewer plant that obliterates the lowest section just above the Schuylkill. If it weren't for the sewer plant, the lowest section could be decent trout water, and maybe there are a few hidden away in there. Basically this is a neat stream that has been killed by "progress."

Valley Creek—6

This stream poses one of the challenges of this project. The county line coincides almost exactly with the edge of the limestone bedrock. However, for about a mile downstream there is flow through a totally different substrate, but the limestone quality of the water persists. The whole stretch is within Valley Forge Park, roughly downstream of the covered bridge.

As the lowest section of the stream, and the fact that it is public property, this area gets much of the pressure. Nevertheless, it is great water, with loads of wild browns, even if they wise up rather quickly and get lockjaw early in the season. They are not easy fish, and the absence of major hatches does make it tougher. But the fish are there, and they have to eat, so they can be fooled.

This is the best stream in Montgomery County, and one of the best in southeast Pennsylvania. Why it doesn't get more attention remains one of the world's mysteries. The knowledge that there are considerable numbers of fish in every speck of decent habitat makes it worth going back.

Wissahickon Creek—7

Near Stenton Avenue on the edge of Philadelphia, which is roughly the end of the limestone area, the stream is maybe 30 feet wide, stocked, and has water around 83 degrees. It may cool off downstream, but that is freestone and in the center of the city. I didn't pursue it downstream.

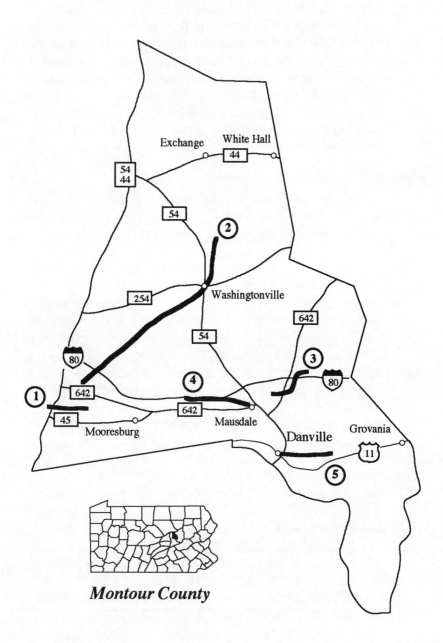

Montour County

MONTOUR COUNTY

In spite of such hopeful signs as Limestone Township and Limestone Ridge as prominent features on the maps, this county really has little limestone influence on its streams. While not an unattractive area to drive through, it is not a memorable area to fish.

Beaver Run—1

This small tributary to Chillisquaque Creek is small and overgrown. It has warm water and no evidence of limestone influence—in spite of being in Limestone Township!

Chillisquaque Creek—2

The 1775 Penn Map shows Tilghmans Springs as the headwaters for this stream that flows through Limestone Township, past Limestone Ridge. Hidden jewel? Nope. This 20- to 30-foot-wide stream shows no signs of limestone influence. Tilghmans Springs proved elusive, and I couldn't find anything special about this stream. No trout turned up and the water was warm. Basically it's not an attractive stream.

Kase Run—3

This small stream is about 7 to 15 feet wide and has some nice holding water. The water is not particularly warm or cold. While there were numbers of *Isonychia* (one of my favorite hatches), there were no trout. This seems to be a freestone chub stream.

Mauses Creek—4

This stream is very similar to the upper portions of Kase and Sechler runs. It is about 10 to 15 feet wide, with little evident limestone influence and less sign of trout, even though the stream is stocked. Loads of chubs, though.

Sechler Run—5

This small stream is channelized in the town of Danville and pretty much devoid of good habitat. I saw some elodea when I was there, but the water was warm, and on the whole uninviting, with no fish in sight. Upstream the water is a little cooler and, of course, the stream is somewhat narrower. There is some nice holding water, which appears to be mainly full of chubs, although I also turned up a smallmouth. Who says streams have to be 30 feet wide to support smallmouths? Anyway, I didn't find any trout.

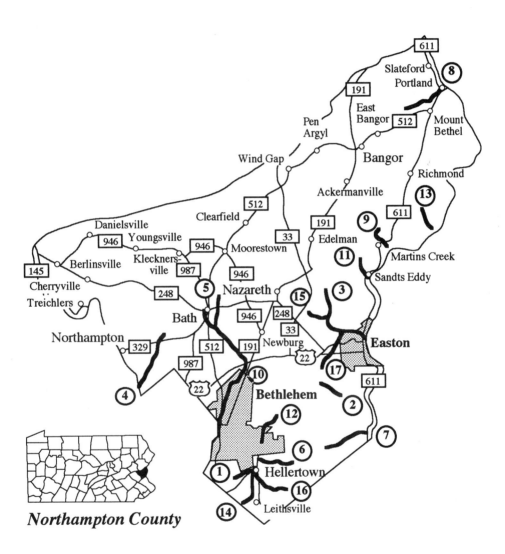

Northampton County

NORTHAMPTON COUNTY

This county represents the eastern edge of the great limestone belt that runs west and south through the center of the Commonwealth. While it is quite densely populated and relatively near even more densely populated areas, it has a number of excellent limestone waters.

There may be some competition between Monocacy Creek and its eastern neighbor the Bushkill as to which is the better water. I'm easy. I don't much care which is better, and I think we are fortunate to have such a choice, as both are limestone waters in the classic sense and great fisheries. Neither is likely to be confused with a wilderness stream, but both streams are doing nicely in spite of the urban setting and the problems that go with it (including a major fish-kill on the Monocacy a few years back caused when a truck filled with detergent flipped on an entry ramp to a major roadway).

If these two streams were the only ones in the county, I would be impressed; but to have a number of others is astounding. Mud Run, Jacoby Creek, Nancy Run, and Saucon Creek—which Lazarus-like has returned from the dead—I recommend them all.

The area is blessed with abundant cold, clean limestone waters. It's also built up and heavily populated, which takes a toll on the aesthetics, but the fish are there. That truck spill on Monocacy Creek has been used to considerable effect to show PennDOT the value of designing to contain potential spills, so perhaps in the long run the damage done to Monocacy Creek can benefit other waters in the state. The Saucon shows signs of returning to its former self, as well. Overall, this county ranks near the top of any list of areas for limestone stream fishing.

Black River—1
I have no idea who gave this miserable ditch that grand name. True, it is a limestone stream, but it is just a storm-water-runoff channel, with a tiny trickle in the bottom. Not trout water!

Bull Run—2
This stream is tiny and not a trout fishery.

Bushkill Creek—3
This is an important stream, with a good population of both wild and stocked brown trout, especially in its lower end, which is the

limestone section. It is quite large, especially in the lower sections around Easton, with large, deep pools (many of which unfortunately are behind dams) and some natural pools hundreds of yards long that appear bottomless. The water temperatures seem to hold relatively well through the summer (mid-60s, perhaps creeping into the 70s during hot spells), no doubt due to springs, as there are not many feeders. It looks like freestone water, but has the temperatures of limestone water.

The lower sections are not overly scenic. Factories detract from the pastoral experience, and I learned long ago that people won't fish beside factories. I do, and I generally find a thriving fish population. Such is the case with the Bushkill.

The upper sections are somewhat gentler, but there appears to be a good gradient throughout, producing some rare habitat, limestone pocket water! The water has excellent clarity making for spooky fish, but they are numerous and in impressive condition. No doubt this stream would be far more famous if not in an urban setting. The fish don't seem to mind (I did not fish below the very large Pfizer plant, which might be a different story). They are picky, hard-fighting fish that are faster to refuse.

It is certainly nice to read the water, locate that imaginary "X" which says there's trout, cast to it, and know with reasonable certainty that indeed a trout is there.

The insect hatches are what you'd expect from classic limestone water. This stream is one of Don Douple's favorites. He suggests the following hatch information covering the major events of the year. Blue-winged Olives can be found midafternoon in early spring, with some caddis a bit later. He thinks the sulphurs are the best hatch of the year, which is often true, running from late May into early June in the evenings, followed by a Light Cahill. Stoneflies turn up in the heavy water, as well as *Isonychia* and *Tricorythodes* (midsummer). There are scuds and cress bugs all the time.

Though this stream doesn't pop to mind when thinking about the spring runs of central Pennsylvania, I found it lovely water to fish. No matter where you start from, it is worth the trip.

Catasauqua Creek—4

This is a nice little stream, maybe 10 to 15 feet wide, with cold water but no trout that I could find. In parts it is a spring creek, with

aquatic vegetation, nice holding water, overhanging vegetation—
the whole bit. Where are the fish?

East Branch Monocacy Creek—5

This small stream, maybe 6 to 10 feet wide, has little decent holding water, lots of filamentous algae, and chubs. No sign of any
trout.

East Branch Saucon Creek—6

This is a nice-looking stream, but it appears to have some thermal
problems. I fished it in early June on an afternoon when the air
was 74 degrees and the water was 77 degrees. I saw no sign of any
trout, and with those water temperatures I doubt there ever will
be. One thing to note is the stream work that PennDOT did here
when building new Interstate 78—a fish passage under a very long
culvert and upstream riprapping to create holding water. If only
the water were not so warm, this could be a charming little
stream.

Frys Run—7

This tiny limestoner flows along the extreme southern border of
Northampton County, over the hill from the much larger Cooks
Creek in Bucks County. There are steep sections of pocket water
where the stream cascades down over limestone outcrops, and
meadow stretches up higher. Nevertheless, it is very small, only
about 5 to 10 feet wide in most places, without any really great
holding water, but with 61-degree temperatures in mid-August.
There is an impressive population of wild browns, enough for the
Fish Commission to manage the stream as a wild trout fishery—
that is, no stocking. It is great to have wild trout in southeastern
Pennsylvania, and this stream makes its contribution. But there
are other, much nicer streams elsewhere in the county.

Jacoby Creek—8

A nice small stream, 15 to 20 feet wide, with heavy pocket water
and stocked fish. While it is in a limestone belt, the boulders in
general are not limestone so I'm not certain how much limestone
influence there is. The trout I caught were stockers, and there
were stoneflies and sulphurs in evidence. Nice stream, if not really memorable.

Martins Creek—9

This is a substantial stream, 30 to 40 feet where it flows across a limestone belt at its terminus with the Delaware River. It is hard to say how much limestone influence this belt gives the stream. I saw numbers of fine trout, but they are probably stockers (12-inch wild brookies are pretty rare in accessible areas). The stocked stream has good pocket water, good runs and pools, and great insect hatches. The bottom is really slippery, and more than once I recovered from the brink of disaster. Another peril—a charging, angry dog—cost me my best fish of the day. Nice stream, even if it isn't much of a limestone stream.

Monocacy Creek—10

This is an important stream, although its suburban and urban setting might turn you off. It supports a great population of wild browns and appears to be making a very rapid comeback from an incident a few years ago when a truck carrying industrial-strength detergent overturned on an entry ramp to Route 22 and spilled its poison into the creek.

It has what classic limestone streams are supposed to have: seductive currents with sipping brown trout and 60-degree water at the end of June. In some sections you'll find old limestone farmhouses and barns and a few ducks paddling around in the stream, not really bothering the fish. You can find fine large wild browns, as well. My best was a 14-incher, probably not bragging size, but a fine fish by any standard.

The management designation in the upper section, above Illicks Mill, has been recently changed to "trophy trout," which means fewer fish are removed, and those must be over 14 inches. This part of the stream is open to fishing year-round (but catch and release only during the closed portion of the year in March and early April). The stream is stocked below Illicks Mill right down through the city of Bethlehem. There are still a number of wild fish present, however, and typical trout-fishing rules are in place. The more restrictive designation was put in place partly to assist in the recovery of the fishery lost in the disastrous spill. And apparently the plan has worked. The numbers of trout continue to increase.

This stream is much loved by the Monocacy Chapter of TU, and they are very fortunate to have such a gem to work with. If this stream didn't flow through so many backyards—and indeed right through downtown Bethlehem—it would be a famous stream. As a fishery it deserves more attention.

Dr. John Hampsey indicates the main fly hatches on the stream are Diptera (midges) March through November, with various *Baetis* hatching nearly as long through the year. Sulphurs are the main mayfly hatch, especially the *Ephemerella dorothea* hatch from mid-May through mid-June, with *Tricorythodes* hatching from midsummer through October or November. Additionally, as a good limestoner, scuds are an important source of nutrition for trout year-round.

Don Douple adds some caddis to the list: April will have both small (size 20) blacks as well as gray-brown caddis in the size 12 to size 14 range. These are followed into May with size 16 green-bodied, tan-winged caddis, and later still in May there are size 20 pink-bodied, tan-winged caddis.

Mud Run—11

It seems that many streams named Mud Run—or various combinations of similar names—turn out to have gin-clear water over a rocky bottom, and this is certainly the case in this diminutive limestoner. It is a small stream, maybe 10 feet wide in most places, and has several vertical sections with the water splashing over large limestone boulders creating pocket water. Higher up it mellows a bit but has nice holding water with pools and riffles and fine wild browns. The stream is colder in the lower reaches than higher up, indicating substantial spring flows. Physically, everything about the stream says freestone, but the stones are all limestone. It is a little gem, and so what if the fish aren't large—they are beautiful, and this is a beautiful little stream.

Nancy Run—12

This productive little stream deserves better than man has chosen to give it. It runs frigid (with water in the upper 50s) in spite of seemingly endless small dams built along it. The problem is that it flows right behind service stations and truck-repair shops, and through residential neighborhoods. These are not the worst places in the world, but they aren't the high-rent district either. Even with this to overcome, the stream has a fine population of wild browns and, apparently, brookies, although I didn't turn up any.

The browns include some of the most gorgeous trout I have ever seen. Golden trout (which I have caught out West and are truly beautiful) might have to share their fame as well as their name with these fish. Gold is the predominant hue, their red spots are crimson, and their fins are an equally bright red. They are impressive!

This is a fine little fishery in the wrong place. Being small (maybe 10 feet wide in general), it clears fast after heavy rains and is worth keeping in mind for times when the larger streams nearby (it lies between the Monocacy and Bushkill) run chocolate.

Oughoughton Creek—13

Flow over limestone bedrock generally upgrades water quality and contributes cold spring water, but in this case the opposite is true. Once this small stream hits the limestone, it simply disappears underground!

Saucon Creek (See Lehigh County, Saucon Creek, page 179.)—14

Schoeneck Creek—15

This is a pretty little limestoner with loads of aquatic weed. It looks like a classic spring creek. The bad news is that the stream has a severe thermal problem, apparently due to the discharge from a quarry and a sewer plant upstream. At present this is not trout water, but maybe sometime in the future it can be brought back.

Silver Creek—16

This stream is very small and flows right through the town of Hellertown, where it meets the Saucon. At the point of confluence it is barely large enough to support a few trout—but it does support large numbers of tires and broken soda bottles. It is an urban stream where it might be large enough to support a fishery. I poked around for a bit and saw no evidence of trout.

Spring Run—17

This small stream, 8 to 15 feet wide, is a mix of the very good and the very bad. The bad is pretty obvious: it is urbanized and suffers from poorly managed storm water and accumulations of trash. This small treasure needs some love. The good news is more subtle and hopeful: the stream runs cold and gin clear and has a very good head of wild browns right in the middle of Easton. Much of the stream runs through a park and is generally under control. In general the fish don't run large, but there are lots of them in good holding water. It is possible to look down into pools and see the trout stacked up like kindling, but they are picky and tough to catch. Their coloration is a bit on the bland side, but hey, this is a great population of wild trout right in the middle of an urban setting. The stream isn't worth a special trip, but since it's a small stream, it probably clears up promptly and is worth keeping in mind if you need to save what otherwise might be a rained-out trip.

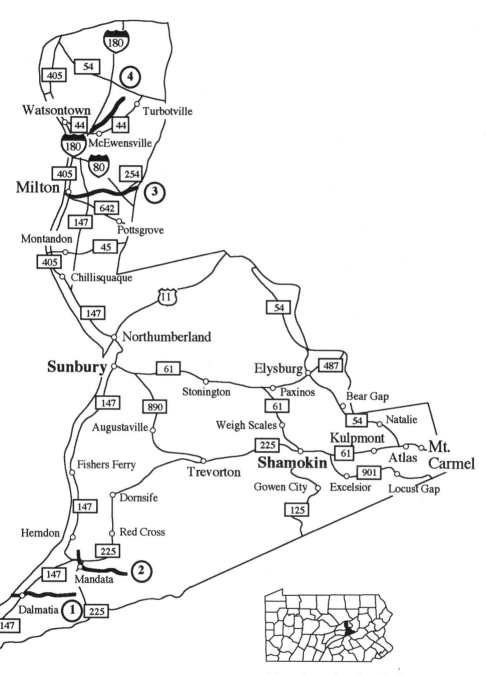

Northumberland County

NORTHUMBERLAND COUNTY

This is definitely a marginal area for limestone outcrops and influence on streams. It isn't totally a zero, but it is no mother lode either.

Perplexing Warrior Run is the only stream which definitely shows limestone influence. If there were a TU chapter in the area, this could be a great piece of water to work with. As it is, this area can safely be left alone in its rural quiet.

Dalmatia Creek—1
This minute stream is barely a trickle, and not a trout fishery.

Fiddlers Run—2
This tiny stream has little going for it. At 3 to 5 feet wide, it should have good cold water, but the temperatures are high (upper 70s) so there is no evident limestone influence or trout habitat.

Limestone Run—3
This small stream has a mouth-watering name, but in reality it is not at all appealing. There is limestone under the stream, and in places there is the right aquatic weed; however, this stream could be a case study titled "Cattle and Their Effects." There is no shade, the banks have been beaten down, it is muddy, it is warm and, as it is now, has nothing to recommend it.

Warrior Run—4
This is a very strange stream. In places it is about 30 feet wide or more and a few inches deep; however, it has good, cool, 68-degree water. In other places it is very deep, far too deep for hippers and, if I had to hazard a guess, probably deep enough to drown in rather easily. It's possible that some of the deep holes are sink-holes (which I had never seen in streambeds, but have spotted a few since then). In places it is absolutely gorgeous trout water but with no evidence of any trout. While there are numbers of chubs, and in places some very large carp, this seems like a great resource going to waste.

Like many limestone spring areas, this region was settled very early and has a remarkable history. During the Revolutionary War it was the scene of a Tory and Indian raid.

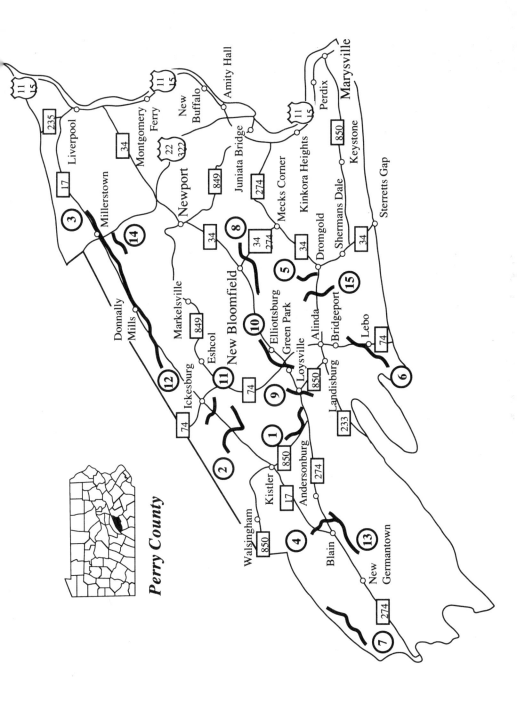

PERRY COUNTY

This particular part of central Pennsylvania generally doesn't have much to offer the angler looking for limestone waters. There are some good areas to drive through, and there are scattered limestone deposits—and some streams in those areas. But there really aren't any memorable limestone streams in Perry County.

Bixler Run—1

This lovely stream is probably a freestone stream, perhaps with some limestone influence. It's about 15 to 20 feet wide, and had 71-degree water in mid-August. Where I was the stream flowed through a hemlock woods and had nice undercut banks, a few log-jams, and some first-rate holding water. I was able to convince only one sublegal wild brown to shake hands with me, but I have no doubts that there are more and larger fish there. The stream is stocked. The fishing wasn't easy, but it was pretty. Even if it is not a limestoner in anything approaching the classic sense, it is a fine small stream.

Buffalo Creek—2

This really appears to be a freestone stream, and with 75-degree water, it has minimal limestone influence. I didn't see any trout, though the stream is supposed to be stocked, but I did manage to rip a gaping hole in my hippers. I was very impressed by the number of wood ducks I saw. It must be dynamite in October!

Cocolamus Creek—3

At Millerstown in mid-August, on a day with 80-degree air temperature, the stream was 81 degrees. It is a decent-sized stream, maybe 30 to 40 feet across, and is probably decent smallmouth water. It does not appear to be a limestone stream.

Conoco Creek—4

This insignificant stream has been under regulation in the past. It is about 3 to 5 feet wide and has warm water, so I guess the special regulations don't really matter. This one is not a leading contender for a position in the top ten.

Falling Spring—5

What a poor imitation of its southern namesake. What's in a name? In this case nothing at all.

Green Valley Run—6

This is a nice stream, up to around 30 feet wide in its lower reaches, with good holding water. There is definite limestone influence (such as the limestone ledges it gurgles over), and while it has the pools and riffles of many meadow streams, it has cool enough water (58 degrees in mid-June) to indicate input from limestone springs. There are deep holes that I had trouble probing with my weighted nymphs. There's a small population of wild browns—the best wild trout fishing in the limestone areas of Perry County—and this pleasant stream is worth keeping in mind if thunderstorms put off the fishing in nearby Cumberland County.

Horse Valley Run—7

This small stream, about 5 to 10 feet wide, certainly appears to be a freestone stream, with no visible limestone influence. While there is little decent holding water, there is a good supply of stocker browns. In mid-August, when I was there, I caught one and terrified the rest. The careless ones were long gone. It is a pretty little stream in a remote valley, but it doesn't appear to have many limestone characteristics.

Little Juniata Creek—8

At Bloomfield this stream is tiny and not a trout fishery.

Loysville Run—9

This pint-sized stream had 78-degree water and very little to recommend it.

Montour Creek—10

With 82-degree water, I felt I had as much information as I needed.

Panther Creek—11

Between Ickesburg and Roseburg the stream is about 15 to 20 feet wide and appears to be a freestone stream, but a few patches of weed give some hint of limestone influence. The water was 71 degrees on a mid-August afternoon, which isn't bad at all. The only trout I caught was a stocker brown, but it was in good shape and gave a good account of itself. There was no evidence of wild fish.

Raccoon Creek—12

At Donnally Mills the stream is small, maybe 10 to 15 feet wide, and has a good number of what appear to be stocker browns. There is evidence of limestone, but this stream can be considered a freestone stream with limestone influence rather than the other way around.

In mid-August the water was 72 degrees and the habitat wasn't overwhelming. I saw no evidence of any natural reproduction, but the stockers I saw certainly had survived in good shape and were able to ignore my clumsy efforts to fool them.

Sherman Creek—13

I visited this stream above the village of Blain, off Three Springs Road, which has an encouraging ring to it. In mid-August the water was 70 degrees, which seemed reasonable for midsummer. However, that's the end of the good news. The stream is almost completely dewatered, with very low flow. It is maybe 25 to 30 feet wide but in a substantially larger streambed. There are some deep pools, and the stream is stocked, but I saw no signs of trout. In general it is very poor, shallow water, and there is no discernible limestone influence. The whole experience was quite a disappointment.

Nevertheless, to give credit where credit is due, a former state-record smallmouth came from the lower stretches of this stream. It is much better suited to smallmouths than to trout.

Sugar Run—14

This stream is essentially dry. The trickle is too small to support minnows.

Warm Spring—15

It is warm indeed, hence of no interest to trout fishers.

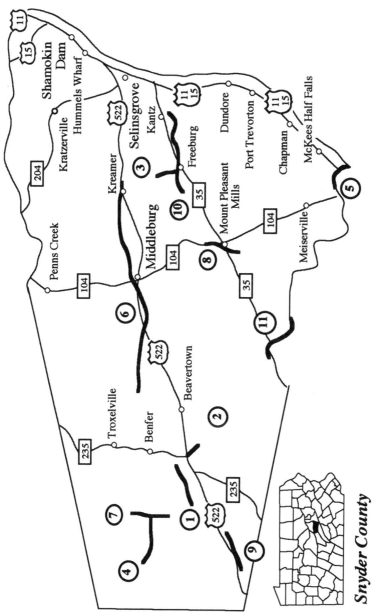

Snyder County

SNYDER COUNTY

This area of central Pennsylvania is dominated by the ridges and valleys that typify the Commonwealth. However, the limestone belts that often run through such areas are, by and large, missing. It is a pretty area to visit, but it is not lush farmland and lacks the prosperity of larger limestone areas. It is unfair to totally write off this county, or adjoining and similar Perry, Juniata, and Union counties. It's just that one may have to search a bit harder to find the limestone-influenced water.

In the case of Snyder County fishing opportunities come down to a few small streams that might be of interest if the larger and more famous streams in the area get muddied by heavy rains. (That comment is aimed specifically at Penns Creek but applies to a few others.) The interesting streams that came to light are small, as befits smaller limestone deposits. There is insufficient critical mass to produce a really big-bang type of limestone stream. Having said all of this, however, it's worth keeping two streams in mind if you need to salvage an otherwise wrecked trip. Kreb Gap Run is small, but it has a substantial number of fish during midsummer and a decent head of fish at other times of the year. North Branch Mahantango Creek is a classic little limestoner, small in size but otherwise very pleasant. Beyond these it's slim pickings.

Beaver Creek—1

This pleasant-looking stream is about 10 to 15 feet wide, but with 84-degree water it is not high on the list of pristine limestone streams.

Beaver Springs—2

This collection of nice little limestone springs would no doubt support a nice fishery except that the village of Beaver Springs has developed right on top of them. In a different location this could be a neat little fishery, but it is pretty well outmatched in this instance.

Dry Run—3

This stream, like the fairly numerous other Dry runs, is well named—and dry.

Kreb Gap Run—4

This is a very strange but interesting stream. It is small, only about 6 to 8 feet wide, and mostly dewatered. The water is not particularly cold at 77 degrees. None of this sounds promising, so I was surprised to find numerous brookies, apparently wild, in several year classes. The fishing is exceptionally tough as the banks are very brushy and, due to dewatering, there are some riffles consisting of exposed rock with only pools holding water. But those pools hold trout in substantial numbers. There are also a few stocker browns which presumably swam up from Middle Creek. The whole place is remarkable. The small size and tough fishing conditions make it nice territory for the small-stream aficionado. There are fish, and that says a lot.

Mahantango Creek—5

With 85-degree water, this is no trout fishery. It looks like good smallmouth water.

Middle Creek—6

At Kreamer, where the limestone is, the stream is about 100 feet wide with 87-degree water. Higher up, at Paxtonville, it is a bit narrower, but the water still is 85 degrees, which creates all sorts of havoc for the stocked trout.

North Branch Kreb Gap Run—7

This is a short (half mile or so) tributary of Kreb Gap Run and is a true limestoner even if small—only 4 to 6 feet wide. It runs cold and is formed by large springs. It has wild brookies and browns, and if they aren't present in huge numbers, they are there in numbers big enough to make this a pleasure to visit. This is a stream to file away and recall if larger streams in the area are muddied up and your trip would otherwise be a total wipeout. After the parade of the other, small, warm-water streams in the county, it is nice to see good habitat.

North Branch Mahantango Creek—8

In an area where there are a number of small limestone lenses, and a number of streams crossing them that lack all appearances of limestone water, this stream is a find! It doesn't rival the Little Lehigh or Fishing Creek, but it is an honest-to-goodness limestone stream with 68-degree water from a large spring located a short distance above Mount Pleasant Mills. It would be wrong to say I saw an incredible number of huge wild browns (the stream is also stocked), but I did turn up a decent number of young of the year, and no doubt with more time and persistence I could have located a few of their parents. This is not an important stream, but in this relatively barren part of the Commonwealth it is worth keeping in mind if you can't fish elsewhere.

South Branch Middle Creek—9
Above McClure this is a tiny, dry streambed.

Susquehecka Creek—10
This small stream flowing near the town of Kantz is yet another alleged limestone stream in an area with little appeal. The limestone lenses appear to be too small to produce much spring flow, so the streams are generally impoverished.

West Branch Mahantango Creek—11
This is a particularly promising-looking stream. Below Richfield it is maybe 15 to 20 feet wide, but warm and apparently with minimal limestone influence. There are loads of minnows, but I could find none of the stocked trout. Not a memorable experience.

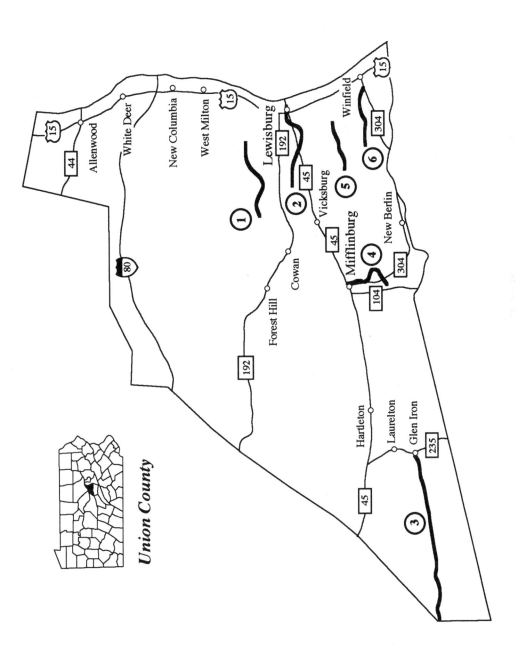

Union County

UNION COUNTY

This is another of those central Pennsylvania counties where there are some small limestone areas and a few small streams with some limestone influence, but, like neighboring Perry and Snyder counties, nothing very exciting. There is one major difference: Penns Creek. While it doesn't flow over limestone beds in Union County, it comes into this area from Centre County carrying a good dose of limestone water, so it brings limestone characteristics into the county. During warm, dry summers Penns Creek might get a bit stressed, but most years it allows good fishing right through the summer doldrums and great fishing when things start to cool off in autumn. In its headwaters area Penns Creek is just another very nice limestone stream, but by the time it gets to Union County it has no competition. If it rains and Penns Creek gets dirty, which it will, leave the county to find alternate water to fish!

Buffalo Creek—1

This large (50 to 60 feet) stocked stream flows across some limestone in the neighborhood of Mazeppa and Kelly Point. It doesn't seem to do the stream any good, though, as it appears to be classic smallmouth water, too warm to hold trout.

Limestone Run—2

What a promising name! This small stream is limestone not only in name but in water quality also. It has lots of large springs feeding it and good cold water. It is virtually in the town of Lewisburg. And at about 10 feet wide, it is a large-enough fishery, if not a great one. Right now it is chub heaven. I didn't handle any trout, although I might have spooked one. The stream has been channelized, but it could be turned into a good fishery with some loving care.

Norman Conrad, Union County's extension agent and an active TU member, says that caddis hatches are so heavy they are considered a nuisance by local residents and businesses. If those residents took better care of their stream, that nuisance could produce a great little fishery.

Penns Creek (See Centre County, Penns Creek, page 88.)—3

Sweitzer Run—4

I was on the stream near Dice, below Mifflinburg. This stream has been trampled flat and is thoroughly uninviting. I saw very little reasonable habitat and almost no characteristics of a limestone stream. Not worth seeking out!

Turtle Creek—5

This small stream seems to have nothing going for it and, in spite of what the geologic maps indicate, does not appear to be a limestone stream. It was running very warm in May and just does not appear to be a trout fishery.

The locals confirmed my evaluation and added a bit. Norman Conrad said, "More like a liquid manure run. It holds a lot of cattle deposits, erosion, silt, and warm water." It won't make any nifty-fifty list!

Winfield Creek—6

This tiny stream flows along a small limestone valley that doesn't seem to do the stream much good. The stream is tiny, not a trout fishery, and not worth further investigation.

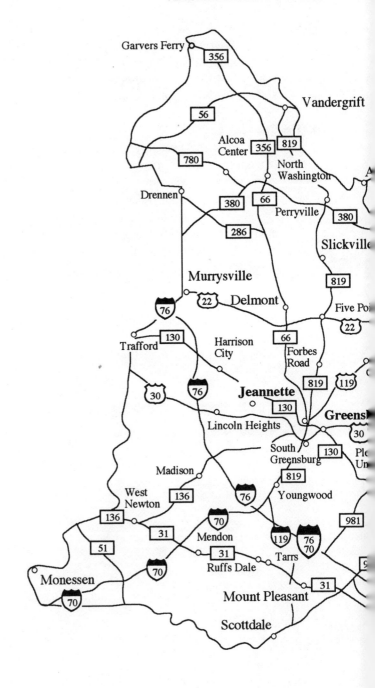

Westmoreland County

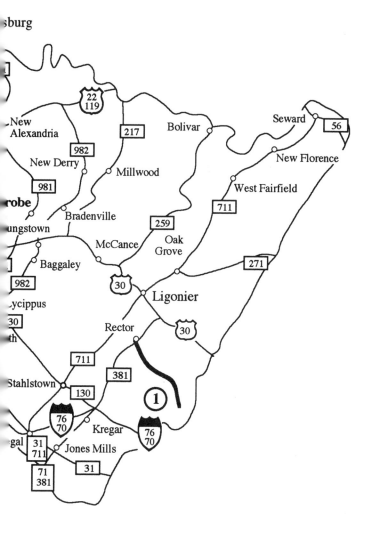

ore

sburg

New Alexandria · 22 119 · 217 · Bolivar · Seward · 56

982 · New Derry · Millwood · New Florence

981 · West Fairfield

robe · Bradenville · 711

ungstown · 259 · McCance · Oak Grove

Baggaley · 982 · 30 · Ligonier · 271

ycippus · 30 · Rector · 30

th · 711 · 381

Stahlstown · 130 · 1

76 70 · Kregar · 76 70

gal · 31 711 · Jones Mills

71 381 · 31

WESTMORELAND COUNTY

Westmoreland is not a county that comes to mind when thinking about limestone areas in Pennsylvania. The only stream listed here, Linn Run, really isn't a limestone stream in any but the most tenuous sense. However, I kept hearing about its name and unique situation, so I arranged a visit. Westmoreland County has been widely mined for coal. Large woods cover most of the county, which has a true western-Pennsylvania feel, quite different from that of the mellower valleys farther east. The frontier days still seem very real here; the edges are not all smoothed over. A pleasant switch from the areas to the east, here the limestone is a relatively thin layer, well buried for the most part.

Linn Run—1

It really is hard to call this pretty stream a limestoner. It runs up to 20 feet wide or so and is a typical freestoner in just about every sense. Its good cool water is the result of many small seeps rather than a jolt from a limestone spring. But there is a definite limestone influence to Linn Run, and therein lies a tale.

Linn Run has acid rain problems. To combat them, wells were drilled deep down into the limestone strata and high-alkali water is pumped up into the stream, dramatically improving its pH and its ability to cope with acid rain.

But there is a twist. The precious buffering water is added to Linn Run only from late spring through early fall, when the stocked trout are present, because budgets don't allow year-round pumping. I suggest running the pumps the other half of the year instead to encourage reproduction of the wild brookies, which are—amazingly—hanging on. The idea is interesting and points out yet another way of using limestone to offset the ravages of acid rain.

Paul Nale points out that this plan may be doing the environment no good because the power to run the well probably comes from burning coal, which means more greenhouse gases, more sulfur dioxide, and other emissions.

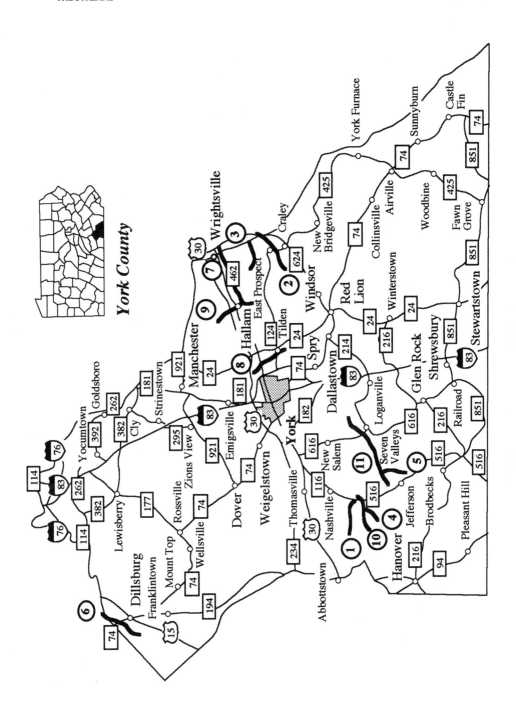

York County

YORK COUNTY

This very pretty county is not endowed with limestone waters, and frankly best represents a pleasant area to drive through on the way to visit its limestone-rich neighbors to the north and west. While some of its streams do show some limestone influence, and some are very attractive looking, none are truly memorable. The county has plenty of lovely old farmsteads, but they don't adjoin luscious spring runs.

Bunch Creek—1

The stream is maybe 8 to 10 feet wide and appears to be a limestone stream. When I was there the water was warm and off-color from rains two weeks earlier, and there were no signs of trout. Not enticing at all.

Cabin Creek—2

This is a good-sized stream, 30 feet or so wide, with nice holding water, some heavy riffles, some pools, and some pocket water. It runs through mature forest and is a pretty stream. The only trout I got my hands on was a definite stocker, and I lost another late in the game. The trout population was sparse. The lowest part of this stream flows through an abandoned limestone quarry which has little influence on the stream.

Canodochly Creek—3

This is a pretty little stream, maybe 10 to 12 feet wide, with limestone ledges. Along the lower end, there are a lot of cottages, which detract from the aesthetics. Up higher it runs through woods and has decent holding water, but no signs of trout. I saw sulphurs and stoneflies when I was there. The only thing missing were trout.

Codorus Creek—4

Above Menges Mills the creek is a pretty meadow stream and good sized at 30 to 50 feet. There are good meander holes, clean gravel, and nice holding water. Apparently it is stocked, but it really looks like smallmouth water. It was very dirty when I was there, although the rains were weeks before. I couldn't buy a trout.

Cold Spring Run—5

A very small, unimpressive stream, it is maybe 6 feet wide and gave no evidence of trout. It was very dirty and warm for early summer. Not inviting.

Dogwood Run—6

This is a pleasant little stream, typically 20 feet wide, with 67-degree temperatures and good holding water. There was no sign of fish of any kind when I visited; however, I do feel there must be some there. If nothing else, this stream must be a summer refuge for thermally stressed fish from the lower Yellow Breeches, into which it flows. It is a nice-looking stream in a nice setting—only the fish appear to be missing.

Kreutz Creek—7

I was on the stream near Yorkana, where it looked like a freestone stream. I didn't see any trout in the 77-degree water. Farther downstream, near Ducktown (great name!), the water was even warmer at 80 degrees. This stream flows through some nice countryside, but it doesn't appear to be much in the way of trout habitat.

Mill Creek—8

The 77-degree water maybe isn't warm enough to be lethal, but sure isn't inviting. The stream has been severely degraded by poor handling of storm water, and it appears to be a dead stream. There are very few chubs and no signs of trout at all.

North Branch Kreutz Creek—9

I was on this nice little stream near the village of Campbell. The water was 69 degrees, which seemed promising; but I didn't move any trout. There might be a remnant population there, nothing grand; this one is up for grabs.

Oil Creek—10

This is a thoroughly forgettable stream. It's about 20 to 30 feet wide but appears lacking in limestone influence. It was very dirty when I visited in spite of the lack of recent rains. I saw numerous carp but no trout. Not worth returning.

South Branch Codorus Creek—11

The limestone area below Seven Valleys is pleasant country, but this stream is not trout water. About 60 feet wide, it gets very muddy when it rains. It might be smallmouth water, but it is not trout water, even though it's supposed to be stocked.

Afterword

So far you have been guided through a wide variety of waters, all bound together by various degrees of limestone influence. Some are simply magnificent, some are terrible, but more tend toward the former than the latter. This is where you enter the picture. Maybe you'll think this is the commercial message and close the book. Please don't—read on.

You've bought this book and read it, so you must be interested in great streams, and being interested means preserving them. Because if you won't, who will?

You may know nothing about Trout Unlimited and how we work, what we do, and what we need. Quite simply the local TU chapters need EVERYONE. No one is too old, too young, too weak, or too anything else that he or she can't help. Being involved doesn't necessarily mean leading the charge against a new sewer plant or landfill. You don't need a formal education in fish management or biology. You don't have to move boulders around creeks to make a better habitat.

I never met anyone who did not have something valuable to offer a TU chapter. Sometimes it's showing up at a township meeting when decisions are about to be made. Sometimes it's licking stamps or labeling newsletters. It can involve writing legislators about upcoming bills which may adversely affect the streams. The list goes on and on. Sure, you're very busy, we all are. But even if you don't have much time, consider giving a little. Get involved. We'll all benefit and so will our lovely Pennsylvania limestone streams.

Pennsylvania Council of Trout Unlimited
P.O. Box 1126
Federal Square Station
Harrisburg, PA 17108

National TU Headquarters
800 Follin Lane, Suite 250
Vienna, VA 22180-4906

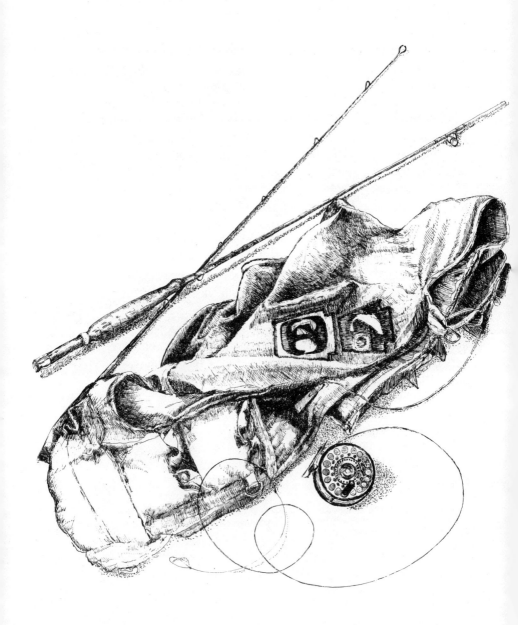

ALPHABETICAL INDEX OF
PENNSYLVANIA'S LIMESTONE STREAMS